Improved Business Planning Using Competitive Intelligence

Improved Business Planning Using Competitive Intelligence

Carolyn M. Vella
and
John J. McGonagle, Jr.

QUORUM BOOKS

NEW YORK
WESTPORT, CONNECTICUT
LONDON

Library of Congress Cataloging-in-Publication Data

Vella, Carolyn M.
  Improved business planning using competitive
intelligence.

  Bibliography: p.
  Includes index.
  1. Business intelligence.   2. Corporate planning.
3. Strategic planning.   I. McGonagle, John J.
II. Title.
HD38.7.V45   1988   658.4′012   88-6012
ISBN 0–89930–340–4 (lib. bdg. : alk. paper)

British Library Cataloguing in Publication Data is available.

Library of Congress Catalog Card Number: 88-6012
ISBN: 0–89930–340–4

First published in 1988 by Quorum Books

Greenwood Press, Inc.
88 Post Road West, Westport, Connecticut   06881

Printed in the United States of America

The paper used in this book complies with the
Permanent Paper Standard issued by the National
Information Standards Organization (Z39.48–1984).

10 9 8 7 6 5 4 3 2 1

Copyright Acknowledgments

Carolyn M. Vella wishes to dedicate this book to
Juanita Hagen Vella, her mother and her friend, and to John,
with love.

John J. McGonagle, Jr. wishes to dedicate this book to
Carolyn, his beloved wife, with love, and to Sassy, the
newest member of his household.

Contents

Preface

In early 1987, a business magazine interviewed a well-known venture capitalist, Frederick A. Adler, about business plans and their shortcomings. Mr. Adler gave his opinions based on his twenty years of experience in evaluating the business plans of companies seeking financial assistance. The interview began as follows:

INC. asked Adler about the warnings in business plans that worry him the most. [He answered:] "Their assumption that if they build a better mousetrap the world will beat a path to their door, rather than that they'll have to go out and find the users of the mousetraps. Lack of details as to competition, direct and indirect [are a major problem in business plans]."

Fortunately, some planning professionals are beginning to recognize the need for Competitive Intelligence (CI) in business planning. But not enough are doing it, and those doing it are not always integrating CI and business planning as thoroughly and quickly as possible.

CI is a vast subject, and all of its aspects cannot be covered in just one book. In this book, we focus on CI and its critical actual and potential contributions to business planning, an area of increasing importance. While this book supplements our 1987 book, *Competitive Intelligence in the Computer Age,* which focuses on CI as it is affected by the increasing availability of computerized data bases, it is designed to stand alone.

This book is not about planning. A lot has been written and said about planning, some of it good, much of it bad. Rather, this book is about improving business planning by injecting CI into the process. To put it in terms of the seminal works on corporate planning by Professor Michael Porter of Harvard, to achieve a competitive advantage, a business must have a competitive strategy. But, and here is the difference, a business cannot develop a sound competitive strategy without adequate competitive intelligence, nor can it expect to apply that strategy and gain any competitive advantages without an ongoing competitive intelligence effort.

Creating and then executing any business plan without CI is like fighting a battle in the dark. You can only guess at your opponent's position. His probable responses to your actions and true strengths and weaknesses are unknown. By the application of brute force your plan may succeed. If you have relied on guesses and your guesses are fairly accurate, you may also prevail.

However, if your adversary has accurate CI about you, your probable intentions, your position, and your strengths and weaknesses, he can turn that intelligence into an advantage. In fact, CI may be an effective substitute for raw economic power.

This book provides an overview of planning in order to stress the importance and proper role of a new and important area, CI. Our approach is to look at types of corporate planning, and provide practical guidance to the readers on how CI can make planning more effective.

STRUCTURE OF THIS BOOK

When we make reference to an on-line data base or other source of data, it is done only to illustrate a point. We are not recommending any particular data base, data source, or vendor. Similarly, if we mention the name of a specific company in an example, that is intended neither as an endorsement nor as a criticism of that company.

To assist our readers, in addition to making each chapter as self-contained as possible, we include a list of key references at the end of each chapter, drawing attention to articles or books of particular relevance to the contents of that chapter. These may help the reader dig more deeply into the topics covered in that chapter. If there are quotations or case studies referred to in the chapter, the references include the source of the quotation or the case study. We have also listed all of the CI case studies by industry in the index. At the end of this book we include a list of additional references of a wider interest. Our references are not intended to be inclusive. Rather they reflect our perception of the most useful materials currently available.

As with our 1987 book *Competitive Intelligence in the Computer Age*, we are including a glossary of key terms. In this book, we define both key CI and planning terms. We also provide four appendices dealing with the CI process as a whole, classifying CI, analyzing competitors and establishing an internal CI unit. These appendices contain cross-cutting materials and can be read by themselves or in connection with topics covered throughout this book.

REFERENCES

"Read This Box, Save $5,000,000," *INC.*, February 1987, p. 61.

Vella, Carolyn M. and John J. McGonagle, Jr., *Competitive Intelligence in the Computer Age*, Westport, Ct: Quorum Books, 1987.

Improved Business Planning Using Competitive Intelligence

1
What Is CI?

COMPETITIVE INTELLIGENCE

Competitive intelligence (CI) is the use of public sources to develop information on competition, competitors, and the market environment. A key precept of CI is that 90 percent of the information that any business needs to make key decisions about itself and to understand its market and competitors is in the public record or can be developed from data already there. Thanks to the computer, and to the thousands of on-line data bases, a whole new meaning has been given to "public."

The use of CI among U.S. businesses is and should be increasing rapidly for a number of reasons. Chief among them is the fact that more and more American businesses realize the importance of CI. These businesses have begun to realize how much information is available. They also see that this information can help them deal directly with their competitors. In addition, some American businesses have come to realize how devastating CI, as developed and used by their competitors, both foreign and domestic, has been. Some have learned only from bitter experience.

Initially, American businesses realized that they did not have adequate information upon which to base their competitive decisions. Because of that, a few first turned to information brokers and, thus, validated an emerging industry. But that new source of raw data was soon seen as insufficient.

At that early point, many American businesses were satisfied to get any competitive data. However, as the quantity of available data increased, companies found that they had to do more than just summarize it to develop a complete and accurate picture of the competition. American businesses began to find that when they got raw data, it could be filled with internal contradictions or, even worse, it could be wrong. Businesses began to understand that a good source for business information did not necessarily contain accurate information. As a result, many American firms began to look for CI specialists to locate competitive data, analyze and evaluate it, draw logical conclusions from it, and prepare it for presentation. The value of using CI professionals became apparent when these companies found that they no longer had to rely upon guesses, or biased or incomplete sources of competitive information. While unevaluated competitive data may be interesting, and at times even useful, modern businesses have found that they need CI to plan what to do. They are now properly relying more upon CI and CI professionals.

Today, all major businesses need good CI to compete, and, in some cases, they need it even to survive. For the largest corporations, CI may constitute one of the most important means of controlling their own activities in numerous markets and in a multiplicity of lines of business. For them CI provides critical information, because, to a very real extent, information is power for such a business.

Medium sized businesses need good CI both in deciding which are their best markets and in defending them. They also need it when they must decide to merge, acquire, or be acquired by another company. Small businesses need good CI just to make it. With the requirements for business loans put on applications by some banks and other sources of venture capital, they probably need good CI to even get started. There are many ways to get data on your competition. Not all of them are conventional or effective. For example, at least two major corporations have been reported to have hired a psychic to give seminars to Senior Management on improving intuitive abilities. Perhaps intuition is an underused corporate resource, but, to paraphrase the military strategist and historian Karl Von Clauswitz, accurate and penetrating CI is a more useful and essential asset for a corporate executive than any talent for intuition.

THE PHASES OF COMPETITIVE INTELLIGENCE

The acquisition and development of CI involves several different phases:

—*Requirements Phase.* In this phase, you both recognize the need for CI and define what CI you need. This means considering what type of issue (strategic or tactical) is motivating the project, what questions are to be answered by the CI, who will be using the CI, and how the CI will be used.

—*Collection Phase.* In this phase, the data needed to develop the CI is systematically acquired. This involves a determination of who should be performing the CI (a separate CI professional, the user of the CI or both), a frank understanding of the constraints on the assignment (time, money, organizational, informational, and legal), identification of the relevant competitor(s), and identification of potential data sources.

—*Processing Phase.* In this phase, the data which has been collected is evaluated and analyzed to transform it into CI. This may involve comparing the information with CI from other sources, integrating it with other CI, or measuring the results of the CI research against predetermined "bench-marks."

—*Dissemination Phase.* In this phase, the CI is distributed, on time, to those who have requested it and, in some cases, to others who may profit from having it. Here, the final form of the CI as well as security may be important considerations.

Chapters 7 through 10 of this book deal with these issues in more detail in the context of business planning. In addition, Appendix A provides a comprehensive outline of the entire CI process, and Appendix D discusses some of the issues involved in establishing an internal CI unit.

CI CASE STUDIES

In the next few pages, we summarize some actual instances where businesses have made effective use of CI developed from on-line data bases. This will help you to understand the broad applications of CI and how effective CI should literally permeate the entire operation of the modern business.

Accounting for Profits

In one reported case, an Accounting Firm's information center used data bases in support of a project focussed on client recruitment in what the Firm regarded as one of its traditional markets, middle-echelon companies and entrepreneurs. The search used two data bases: one summarized articles on business practices, corporate strategies, and trends from business and management journals, and the other indexed articles from major national newspapers.

The search, which was designed to retrieve data on marketing strategies of the Firm's competitors, located several references to the Firm's chief competitors by name. The Firm found that its Big Eight competitors were actively soliciting new accounts. This raw information was in turn passed on to company analysts who organized it into a report for senior management. When senior management saw how aggressive its Big Eight competitors were becoming, it decided to market and sell its own services more aggressively. The result was an increase in market share for the Firm.

The Phantom Price War

In another context, a Consumer Products Corporation was alerted to a trade rumor that a competitor was preparing to take on one market which the Corporation had had to itself for a long time. The Corporation prepared to cut its prices in advance of the expected marketing initiative in an effort to defuse the expected campaign. However, before price cuts were put into place, the Consumer Products Corporation had a CI report prepared on this particular competitor. On-line research disclosed that the competitor had been purchased by a conglomerate several years earlier. On-line review of advertising publications and local newspapers did not show any indication that the competitor had recently hired a new advertising agency, which might have indicated the advent of a new marketing campaign.

Additional on-line research disclosed that the competitor's parent corporation had tried to sell the competitor because it was not profitable. Another story indicated that the rating of the parent's commercial paper was being downgraded. It also mentioned the threat of lawsuits by debenture holders.

A business news data base showed that a key senior executive of the competitor's parent corporation had recently retired and that no successor had yet been appointed. The result was that the competitor's parent corporation was potentially leaderless. Finally, other stories hinted at internal turmoil at the parent corporation level in the wake of other executive departures.

In light of these findings, the Consumer Products Corporation decided that what seemed to be a dangerous threat to a protected market was at most a gesture by a competitor which was probably not in a position to undertake a new, costly marketing campaign of the type necessary to threaten the protected market. This meant, in turn, that the anticipatory price cuts were not necessary.

Food for Thought

CI research does not have to cover a wide range of subjects to produce information of importance to a business. For example, when researchers at a major Food Company heard a rumor that a prime competitor was offering a new frozen food line, it turned to on-line data bases to verify the rumor.

Conducting an on-line search under the name of the new product, the Food Company found the product mentioned in transcripts of a new products conference that had been held the day before. In light of this, the Food Company immediately began to plan its response. CI, relying on on-line data bases, permitted a more rapid response to a new product than had been possible in the past.

REFERENCES

McDonough, Michael, "Psychics in the Mainstream," *Woman's World*, March 31, 1987, pp. 6–7.

McKie, Peter, "Tracking Your Competition—The Online Edge," *Personal Computing*, May 1986, pp. 93–103.

Miller, Tim, "Staying Alive In The Jungle," *Online Access Guide*, March/April 1987, pp. 44–57.

Prescott, John E. and John H. Grant, "Manager's Guide to Competitive Analysis Techniques," Graduate School of Business, University of Pittsburgh, May 1986. An overview of a variety of financially-oriented competitor analysis techniques. Of particular interest is a table comparing 21 different techniques in areas such as scope, resource needs, data needs, accuracy constraints, and updating requirements.

Vella, Carolyn M. and John J. McGonagle, Jr., *Competitive Intelligence in the Computer Age*, Westport, Ct: Quorum Books, 1987. This book focuses on introducing businesses to the wide variety and effective utilization of data available from on-line data bases.

2

An Overview of Business Planning

WHAT IS BUSINESS PLANNING?

The term "planning" has no precise and generally accepted meaning in business. In some business contexts, it is used to cover all management techniques which deal with any future event. In others, its meaning is closer to "scheduling." As used in the modern corporation, its meaning lies somewhere in between.

One classic definition of business planning was given almost 30 years ago by Peter Drucker:

[P]lanning is the continuing process of making present entrepreneurial decisions systematically and with the best possible knowledge of their futurity, organizing systematically the efforts needed to carry out these decisions, and measuring the results of these decisions against the expectations through organized, systematic feedback.

Another, more modern, definition of business planning is the following:

[T]he analysis of relevant information from the present and past and an assessment of probable future development so that a course of action (plan) may be determined that enables the organization to meet its stated objectives.

For the purposes of this book, we adopt a consensus definition of planning as follows:

Planning is a process by which the mission of a business organization is defined, its competitive strengths, including resources and liabilities, are evaluated, its goals are established, its alternative courses of action identified and selections made from among them, and the programs, projects, and tasks necessary to achieving those goals are determined.

Regardless of the exact academic definition of "planning," what is clear is that planning is a process, and one which is not limited to any particular type of business plan. It involves both obtaining needed information and deciding on a course of action which reflects that information, among other factors. In practical terms, planning is the process of making decisions and selections, and planning problems arise only when there are decisions to be made or options from among which a selection must be made.

In modern business, planning is one of the three key elements of the process of management, these elements being: planning, directing, and controlling.

— *Planning.* setting objectives, gathering and analyzing data, developing alternatives, preparing plans of action, and selecting from among the alternatives available to accomplish the plan's objectives.

— *Directing.* attaining the organization's objectives by using management tools, such as organization, communication, and decision-making.

—*Controlling.* measuring progress, evaluating actions, and taking corrective action to identify and modify the organization's performance and adherence to the plan. It also involves providing continual feedback to the planning element to improve the overall management process.

WHY IS PLANNING IMPORTANT?

The single most important reason for planning is that it helps the business executive avoid management by reaction or by inaction. Planning does not guarantee that a business can influence events and be positioned to quickly respond to changes in the marketplace. However, the lack of planning can virtually assure that the business will be reactive and unable to respond.

As Sun Tzu said in the context of warfare,

He who has a thorough knowledge of his own conditions as well as of the conditions of the enemy is sure to win in all battles. He who has a thorough knowledge of his own conditions but not the conditions of the enemy has an even chance of winning and losing a battle. He who has neither a thorough knowledge of his own conditions nor of the enemy's is sure to lose in every battle.

In general terms, planning provides critical assistance in several specific ways:

Planning directs the attention of management and staff to the business' objectives. The process of planning focuses attention on deciding what are the objectives of the business as well as on the strategic and tactical factors involved in accomplishing those objectives. In fact, some believe the very process of planning is important, regardless of the actual plan produced. According to one venture capitalist who describes most business plans he sees as "still lousy,"

The benefit of a business plan comes in the writing...when the founders think through their strategies. "It's a good discipline to get together the staffing requirements, specifics of the product plan, specifics of the marketing plan."

Planning helps a business prepare for the future as well as deal with the present. Since the future is unknown, and often characterized by rapid and unexpected changes, an executive must be alerted to the need for necessary changes in business operations as the future becomes clearer. Only by having previously considered the future and its impact on present operations can an executive consistently hope to be able to recognize that events are happening which may require strategic or tactical changes and to know what those changes are.

Planning helps to minimize unnecessary costs. By concentrating attention on options facing a business in the light of probable and even possible future events, planning tends to assist in identifying and then selecting the best and most cost-effective of available options. There are few courses of action which are less cost-effective and more likely to fail than ad hoc responses to new developments.

Planning helps provide true control over operations. Control without a defined purpose or objective is difficult, if not impossible. It becomes regimentation without a purpose and ultimately develops into regimentation for the sake of regimentation. By defining an agreed-upon and understood set of objectives for the business, planning provides a bench mark against which performance can be measured and towards which an organization can be directed.

BASIC REQUIREMENTS OF PLANNING

Effective business planning requires more than a mere procedure or directive requiring all managers to "come up with a plan." Rather, the process requires at a minimum the following:

—*Planning must be used by senior management.* To be effective, the planning process must not only be supported by, but also used by, top management. If senior management does not rely on the process and results of business planning for its decision-making, then management's ability to insist on compliance with a plan ultimately diminishes. When management, supervisors, and employees come to believe that their actions are not being held accountable on a consistent basis to the goals and objectives of the plan, the process ultimately becomes a merely sterile exercise in research, data collection, and memo writing. Just as control without planning results in chaos, planning without related control results in stagnation.

—*Planning is unique.* While management of a business involves many interdependent functions, planning is both a part of and apart from management. It is a part of management in that it sets the goals necessary for the business' actions. However, it is simultaneously apart from management in that it is a continuing process, continuing regardless of current operations and styles of management.

—*Planning must contribute to attaining objectives instead of just identifying them.* While it is essential that planning identify the competitive environment and set business objectives, it must do more than that. It must identify the means of accomplishing those objectives and establish ways to determine whether or not those goals have been met and why there are any deviations from the goals. In short, planning must be realistic and useable.

—*Planning must be pervasive and persuasive.* Effective planning must involve all levels of management. Those involved in monitoring the progress of a business under a plan must always be careful that managers do not mentally separate planning from "operations." Managers must be persuaded that planning is an integral element of all operations, and that their operations must provide continual feedback to the planning process. To accomplish this, the plan and its objectives must be widely disseminated within a business. While it may not always be possible or even desirable for all aspects of a business plan to be publicized, the principal policies, premises, objectives, and other critical elements of the business' plan should be known to those made responsible for carrying it out.

—*Planning and implementing plans take time.* The time span allotted for the planning process, which ideally should repeat itself at least each year, should be long enough to allow adequate consideration and coordination of all the steps involved. But, it must not be permitted to extend over so long a time as to make it meaningless. Setting up the planning process so that it can accept new data and assumptions helps balance the need for work that may take over a year to complete from the initial step but which must be up-to-date when presented. Similarly, the period for which a plan is prepared will vary. For example, in some industries, a five-to-ten-year plan may be appropriate, particularly when decisions must be made about major capital expenditures. In other industries, however, rapidly changing technology or consumption patterns may make meaningless any plan which covers more than two years.

THE PLANNING PROCESS

The planning process involves a number of key steps, but, unlike many other processes, such as those in manufacturing, these steps do not proceed in order. Planning involves continual feedback between and among its own steps. The core elements of business planning are as follows:

1. Identifying opportunities
2. Selecting objectives
3. Establishing the business context
4. Identifying options
5. Evaluating options
6. Selecting or modifying options
7. Establishing or modifying supporting plans:
   —corporate strategies
   —policies
   —procedures

—rules
—programs
—budgets
—other Related Business Plans

8. Disseminating the plan
9. Initiating the plan
10. Implementing the plan
11. Evaluating the plan's progress
12. Obtaining feedback and updating the plan

Among the most critical of the procedures followed in any business planning process are the following:

—*Set appropriate and identifiable objectives.* In setting goals, or targets, or objectives, however they are labelled, determine if they are to be expressed quantitatively or qualitatively. If, for example, the goals can be expressed as a quantity or a number, then you can make the goal into a standard, such as a 34 percent reduction in defects. However, not all goals can be expressed as a number. If you are setting a qualitative goal, determine how you can monitor progress towards that goal. A goal is not appropriate if you cannot discern if there has been progress towards (or away) from it. This means that a stirring objective such as "improved customer satisfaction," without any concrete way to determine if customers are more satisfied, is not an appropriate objective.

The plan's objectives should meet the following standards:

1. They should be able to be achieved as a result of the planning process;
2. they should be feasible and acceptable in relation to the costs involved in achieving them;
3. they should be compatible with other business objectives.

—*Establish a clear purpose for the plan.* This involves realizing that planning has two elements, the process and the product. Depending on the purpose of the plan, one may be more important than the other. Among other issues, you must establish who is the plan's ultimate audience. For example, you may prepare a different plan for obtaining outside financing than you would to determine a target for a joint venture. It is not that the conclusions differ, but that the final form of the product may differ.

—*Research and analyze.* An important step in the planning process is to make an adequate analysis of the problem or problems which the business faces. This typically involves refining the objectives to be achieved, identifying major obstacles to be overcome, obtaining and evaluating data on past, present, and future competitive conditions which affect the business and attaining the objective, and forecasting future events or constructing competitive scenarios to provide a background against which options and their impacts can be evaluated.

—*Identify and test assumptions.* You should always be clear about what you take as a "given" in the planning process. First, if you cannot clearly articulate a premise, you should question whether it should be accepted at all. Second, in setting forth the premises underlying any business plan, you avoid any hidden agendas. Third, you may find that what you have always accepted as "given" is not so, or may no longer hold true for the period the plan covers.

—*Articulate the elements of the plan.* The business' objectives and the steps needed to achieve them should be clearly specified and identified. The options available for action should be spelled out, and the costs and related consequences of each should be clear.

—*Search for possible solutions.* One way to find solutions for problems raised in the planning process is to break the objective or goal into a set of subgoals. Each subgoal in turn becomes one of the means of achieving the primary goal. In turn, each subgoal may be broken down into more detailed goals which, when accomplished, lead to the achievement of the subgoals. Using this process may help break a complex, and seemingly insoluble, problem into a set of smaller problems, each of which can be solved on its own. Alternatively, it may disclose that the problem raised by the planning process is in fact insoluble, and that some other objective must be adopted by the business. In either case, the planning process has made an invaluable contribution to the business' welfare. Once possible solutions have been identified, you should measure them and the means required to achieve them against other business objectives. You should also determine if they can be accomplished within any constraints imposed by available resources of the business, such as funds or manpower. Then, check all of the steps in each solution for internal inconsistency and impracticability. While it would be ideal to analyze all of the consequences of each alternative in detail, this is probably not feasible, because this would turn the planning process into a never-ending process of reviewing small steps, and it would eventually mean losing sight of the business' principal objectives. However, you can select out the alternatives to a few of the most likely consequences and then review each of them in some detail.

—*Compare alternatives.* Within the business plan, you may, and perhaps should, have several sets of alternatives to consider. One level of comparison may be to identify and then resolve inconsistent or even contradictory objectives. Another may be to check the analyses themselves for internal errors or weaknesses. Yet another might involve testing one option for a limited time and in a limited arena before adopting it for the entire business.

—*Match means and objectives.* The objectives sought and the means required to achieve them should be matched. This should be done both in terms of the relationship between the means required for an individual objective as well as in terms of the impact of the means selected on the business as a whole. For example, while allocating a set amount of funds to achieve a given business objective may appear appropriate, that allocation might result in taking away funds available to support other objectives. In that case, a decision must be made as to relative priorities before either objective is adopted and steps taken to implement it.

—*Identify actions and commitments needed.* The actions needed to achieve each objective should be specific, feasible, and acceptable. This means deciding if the objective can actually be accomplished and determining whether the cost of taking the necessary steps is acceptable. When you do this, you will later be able to determine whether the actions have been taken as well as whether the related objectives have been attained. The actions and commitments needed should represent a decision to proceed, and should not merely list options.

—*Be practical and realistic.* You must realize that you cannot quantify everything. In some cases, the "spreadsheet' syndrome takes over. Among other things, that means that many businesses substitute the generation of numbers for the discipline of answering questions.

REFERENCES

Drucker, Peter F., "Long-Range Planning—Challenge to Management Science," *Management Science*, April 1959, pp. 238–49.

Larson, Erik, "The Best-Laid Plans," *Inc.*, February 1987, pp. 60–64. A discussion of instances when planning was not followed and its consequences.

Sisk, Henry L., *Management and Organization* (3rd ed.), Cincinnati: Southwestern Publishing Co., 1977. Chapter 4 provides a workable view of planning in action.

Sun Tzu, *The Art of War*, New York: Oxford Press, 1963, p. 82, as quoted in Howard H. Stevenson, "Resource Assessment: Identifying Corporate Strengths and Weaknesses," William D. Guth (ed.), *Handbook of Business Strategy*, Boston: Warren Gorham & Lamont, 1985.

3

How Can CI Help Planners and Planning?

WHY DOES BUSINESS PLANNING REQUIRE CI?

Since its growth period in the 1970s, the development of corporate planning has fallen on hard times in many industries. In part, this reflects the decision of some businesses to cut current expenses to produce immediate improvements in bottom-line performance. Because of this, corporate planning at many levels has been hit by cost reductions resulting from such pressures. It has been hit particularly hard when the corporation decides to cut expenses principally from staff, not line functions. Of course, such cuts are often short-sighted, since they involve trading off immediate small gains in profitability for increased vulnerability in the future, due to the reduction or elimination of effective corporate planning.

In some circles, corporate planning, particularly strategic planning, has come to be regarded as too academic or too remote from reality. In part, this may reflect a focus by some planners on the process of planning while neglecting to make that planning applicable to real corporate situations. In general, too many corporate plans, particularly those developed for competitive strategies, are based on limited information about competitors and the competitive environment, or worse, on one or more of the following erroneous, but very common, assumptions in place of accurate data:

—A firm's competitors will continue to act in the future as they have in the past.

—Every competitor, in any given situation, will behave just as this firm would.

—Competitors know everything our firm knows, but nothing more.

—All of our competitors perceive the market in the same way our firm perceives it.

Today, the business plans which are most successful are those based upon and using competitive intelligence. Professor Michael Porter of Harvard puts it this way:

Knowledge of these underlying sources of competitive pressures provides the groundwork for a strategic agenda of action. They highlight the strengths and weaknesses of the company, animate the positioning of the company in its industry, clarify the areas where strategic changes may yield the greatest payoff, and highlight the places where industry trends promise to hold the greatest significance as either opportunities or threats....

Every industry has an underlying structure, or a set of fundamental economic and technical characteristics, that gives rise to these competitive forces. The strategist, wanting to position his company to cope best with its industry environment or to influence that environment in the company's favor, must learn what makes the environment tick....

Once the corporate strategist has assessed the forces affecting competition in his industry and their underlying causes, he can identify his company's strengths and weaknesses.

WHERE CAN CI FIT INTO
PLANNING AND STRATEGY?

CI can fit almost anywhere and should be used almost everywhere. Paraphrasing Nicollo Machiavelli in the context of competition:

An executive should never, therefore, have out of his thoughts this subject of competition, and when there is no significant competition, he should addict himself more to its exercise than when there is direct competition. This he can do in two ways, the one by action the other by study.

As regards action, he ought above all things to keep his personnel well organized and practiced, by which he accustoms himself to hard work and learns something about the nature of his own markets and company.... [w]hich knowledge is useful in two ways. First, he learns to know his own market and is better able to undertake its defense. Afterwards, by means of the knowledge and observation of that market, he understands with ease any other which it may be necessary for him to study thereafter... so that with a knowledge of the aspect of one corporation or market one can easily arrive at a knowledge of others. And the executive that lacks this skill lacks the essential which it is desirable that a leader should possess, for it teaches him to surprise his adversary, to select defense positions, to direct his personnel, to engage in competition, to assault markets to advantage.

[T]o exercise the intellect the executive should read case studies, and study there the actions of illustrious executives, to see how they have borne themselves in competition, to examine the causes of their victories and defeat, so as to avoid the latter and imitate the former.

For example, the potential importance of CI in marketing plans alone can be seen in data collected about the origins of new product ideas. According to one survey, the largest source of new product ideas for consumer products was an analysis of the competition. This was true in 38.0 percent of the cases. Published information provided the new idea in 11.4 percent of the cases.

For industrial products, the same survey showed that an analysis of the competition, cited in 27.0 percent of the cases, was the second most productive source of new product ideas. In addition, published information was responsible for the new product idea in 7.9 percent of the cases. Thus, effective CI can provide a significant source of new product ideas for marketing planners.

Developing Businesses

CI is a necessary adjunct to planning even in the start-up of businesses. The experience of those who provide funding for developing businesses is clear—the key to acquiring venture capital is to have a solid, realistic, and intelligible business plan. That plan should frankly assess both the capabilities of the entrepreneurs and the market and competition which those entrepreneurs face.

Just where does CI fit in the scheme of things for developing businesses? Actually, it should fit everywhere. Many, but not all, established businesses, particularly those in high and medium technology industries, engage in some degree of CI at many levels. Use of CI can range from the simple tracking of new product introductions to sophisticated analysis of likely internal cost structures of potential competitors.

The developing business, particularly one which lacks unlimited financial and technological resources, must use CI if it hopes to keep even and, more importantly, if it plans to get ahead. To put it in a nutshell—a developing business must plan to grow and survive. To plan, a developing business must have information on its competition, actual and potential, and on its markets, both current and future. And, to have information on these subjects, a developing business must use CI.

This bears repeating. Every business must plan, but this is most important for the developing business. That is because the developing business does not have the historical inertia and financial momentum to carry it forward in the absence of continual and aggressive planning. Now this is not always bad. That means the developing business cannot make the mistakes that the more established firm can make when it fails to make a decision. But the price to the developing business of failing to decide, a consequence of failing to plan, is to do nothing. For the established firm, the consequence is that it continues ahead on a straight line, which may in fact be a good course for a short time. The established firm can afford to get away without planning—once in a while. However, the developing firm can never afford not to plan. The developing firm must plan, moreover, not just for its own benefit but to satisfy those to whom it turns for outside financing.

As those providing equity to developing businesses have affirmed, one of the most frequent shortcomings of the company seeking financial assistance is the lack of a complete and realistic business plan. And one of the most common shortcomings of the business plan, when there is one, is the lack of sound, current information on a firm's competitors and potential competitors. To put it more bluntly, no one will provide equity capital to a business that does not know where it is and where it is going.

Another reason for planning, particularly for the developing business, is to generate and to manage growth. A good idea can result in uncontrolled growth if the owners of the business are not ready for it. And how can they be prepared for it if they do not understand their own market? For example, if your product's future sales growth depends on the installed base of a certain kind of industrial equipment, are you prepared for the growth in your sales that a halving of the price for that equipment will generate? You cannot be if you do not even suspect that such a price change could be coming as it has with computers.

On the down side, planning should also be used to prepare to repulse new competition. Merely because a developing firm has invented a new technology does not guarantee that it will always monopolize the market. A development in another technological area may quickly put that firm out of business.

For example, the authors attended a meeting where an executive of one firm proudly summarized his firm's extensive study of competitor challenges to a new product, one involved in control devices. However, the very next speaker then outlined his firm's findings about Japanese research and development in an entirely different area. When the first speaker asked whether the Japanese research might affect his controls project, the second speaker indicated that yes, in fact, that area was completely encompassed by the new research. The second speaker was then asked what this new research would mean. The curt response was that "Unless you can make your product small enough to fit on the head of a pin, it will be obsolete!" This later proved to be true.

None of the data used by either speaker was confidential. In fact, everything the second speaker referred to was public information—in Japan. But effective and wide-ranging CI efforts by the first speaker could have easily developed the same information.

Established Businesses

One mistake too often made in planning departments of the larger businesses is to assume that CI is already in use at the subsidiary or lower level. In many large decentralized corporations, headquarters management assumes that the operating units routinely monitor key competitors and that their business, marketing, and other plans take into account the current activities of and probable future responses of important competitors. Sadly, that assumption is too often wrong.

For a number of reasons, including the following, planners in larger, decentralized operations neglect to seek and apply CI in their planning:

—They lack the resources to take on more than the routine marginal observations of competitors through regular business reading.

—Their key competitors are themselves part of larger organizations, so that operating level personnel assume that headquarters personnel is tracking them as a part of their responsibilities.

—Headquarters has never made it clear that the identification of likely responses by competitors to corporate plans should be an element of each business or marketing plan.

WHAT KINDS OF CI
ARE AVAILABLE FOR PLANNERS?

Those involved in developing or using business plans of any sort should be more sensitive than most to the importance of accurate and current data, particularly on competitors. But CI opens a world of new current information for those developing business plans.

The richness of data on businesses and business experiences virtually mandates that an executive who wishes to survive in the 1990s and beyond must find it and use it. But the vast scope of such data requires new techniques in formulation of the scope and direction of your research, in the way in which that research is conducted, and in the way the riches of data are mined to provide valuable information.

The vast amount of data which is out in the public domain may be illustrated by the example of problems facing the U.S. pharmaceutical industry overseas. According to industry sources, drug "piracy" is a severe problem in many industrialized nations. Foreign "pirates" obtain information on American drugs from a number of sources, including patents and the files of the U.S. Food and Drug Administration, which reportedly received 34,000 FOIA (Freedom of Information Act) requests in 1982 (the last year for which data is available). As the President of the Pharmaceutical Manufacturers Association put it, these pirates can copy new drugs "faster than we can get them into the market because all the data about a drug is published."

CI has evolved in response to the need to manage and exploit this new wave of data. Using CI enables planners to find masses of data and to turn it into useful information. It is a process to supplement the work of those in corporate planning and competitive strategy development as well as those in related areas such as market research, business development, and product development. CI provides information, developed from a mass of often conflicting data, evaluated for accuracy and reliability.

CATEGORIZING BUSINESS PLANS

There have been many efforts made to categorize business plans. Some observers have divided them according to their duration, that is distinguishing between long-range and short-range plans. Others prefer to classify them according to their scope and level of detail, contrasting strategic with tactical or operational plans. Others distinguish among them according to which level of the business they affect. They differentiate among plans at the corporate level, at the level of the individual line of business, or at a lower level, sometimes called the functional level. Still others classify business plans by which function they most directly impact. Thus they may contrast plans affecting marketing from those impacting production, personnel, new business development, or finance.

In fact, the authors believe that business planning is a process which has many common elements. Further, regardless of the classification or classifications which you adopt to divide business plans, all types of business plans can be grouped under any of the other classifications. For example, if you classify plans by what business function they impact, you can, in turn, reclassify them according to scope and level of detail, as well as by the level of activity affected. The following table illustrates this.

TABLE 1
Categories of Business Plans

```
                    TYPE OF PLAN
         --------------------------------------:
LEVEL OF      :              :                 :
ACTIVITY      : STRATEGIC    :   TACTICAL      :
         -----:--------------:-----------------:
CORPORATE : A,B,C,J,P        :   ++++++++      :
         -----:--------------:-----------------:
LINE OF       :              :                 :
BUSINESS  : C,D,J,L,N        :   A,M,P,R,T     :
         -----:--------------:-----------------:
FUNCTIONAL : ++++++++++      :   A,B,D,L,M,N,T,P :
         --------------------------------------:
```

Key: Specific Types of Business Plans

A. Acquistion/Divestiture Plan

B. Business Development Plan

C. Capital/Financial Planning

D. Plan to Develop the Results of Technical Research

J. Joint Venture Plan

L. Licensing/Technology Transfer Plan

M. Marketing/Sales Plan

N. New Product/Service Development Plan

P. Personnel Development Plan

T. Technical Research Plan

Applying this categorization, you can see in Table 2 how the CI needs of various types of business plans can be classified. Of course, you can convert this table to one specifying the CI needs of plans covering any particular business function by reference to Table 1.

Chapters 4 through 6 cover how to find data and process it into meaningful CI. Chapter 7 and beyond show you specifically where that CI can fit into your planning process.

TABLE 2
Most Common CI Needs

```
                    TYPE OF PLAN
            :------------------:------------------:
LEVEL OF    : STRATEGIC        : TACTICAL         :
ACTIVITY    :                  :                  :
            :------------------:------------------:
            :                  :                  :
CORPORATE   : MACRO-HISTORIC : ++++++++           :
            :------------------:------------------:
LINE OF     :                  :                  :
BUSINESS    : MACRO-CURRENT    : MICRO-HISTORIC :
            :------------------:------------------:
FUNCTIONAL  : ++++++++++++++ : MICRO-CURRENT   :
            :------------------:------------------:
```

Macro. Macro-level data is of a high level of aggregation, such as the size of a particular market, i.e., consumer electronics, or the overall rate of growth of the economy.

Micro. Micro-level data is of a low level of aggregation or even unaggregated data. This might be data, for example, on a particular competitor's company or division profitability.

Historic. Historic data covers a long period of time. It is designed to show long-term trends, such as gross sales in an industry over a five-year period. This may include projections covering a long period of years.

Current. Current data deals with a relatively short period of time, centered on the present. Examples of this might be sales figures for the past three-month period for one competitor.

REFERENCES

Elias, Christopher, "Big Profits, Extensive Research Are Industry's Best Medicine," *Insight,* August 24, 1987, pp. 38–40. This article studies the American pharmaceutical industry's research efforts and problems with overseas "pirating."

Lainson, Susan, *Crash Course,* New York: Ballantine Books, 1985.

Machiavelli, Nicollo, *The Prince,* trans. W.K. Marriott, 1958, Chapter 14. "That Which Concerns A Prince On The Subject Of The Art Of War," Everyman's Library, New York: 1958.

Porter, Michael E., "How Competitive Forces Shape Strategy," *Harvard Business Review*, March/April 1979, pp. 137–145.

Wirth, Paul, "Venture capitalist offers tips to entrepreneurs," *The Morning Call*, March 17, 1987, p. B7.

4
Gathering Data

TREATING DATA AS A COMMODITY

Who Has an Interest in the Data?

One way to determine where the data you need for CI may be is to consider who already has an interest in having that data on a one-time or on a regular basis. This could lead you to government regulatory bodies, trade associations, academics, or, in the case of publicly-traded companies, investment analysts. Each of these sources has data of different types and quality. The type and quality of that data depends on why each collected the data in the first place.

For example, investment analysts are often privy to information which differs from that made available to the press, including the financial press. They may receive financial and marketing strategy briefings which the business press does not receive. The question then arises, how can you access the data they receive? There are at least three ways to do this:

1. Obtain copies of the reports and studies which these analysts prepare based on the presentations.
2. Contact the company involved and ask for a copy of any briefing which it has given to its analysts. This may or may not produce materials. Some corporations will cheerfully provide these; others will have little or nothing to provide.
3. Check sources, both on-line and off-line, such as the Wall Street Transcript, which provides summaries or even the full text of these briefings.

Of course, there is at least one other option—interview the analyst directly.

Sources versus Providers

In treating data as a commodity, keep in mind that where you get the data is not necessarily the ultimate source of that data. While the techniques and issues involved in the analysis of data are discussed in detail in Chapters 5 and 6, an example of the danger of confusing the provider of the data with the source of the data may be instructive here.

In 1986 and 1987, a 27 year-old Pennsylvania man allegedly obtained "almost unlimited credit" from five banks using a Dun & Bradstreet rating based on false information about himself and his business which he supplied to Dun & Bradstreet. According to federal officials, his company was reported as being worth over $40 million when in fact it was never even an operating company and never had "any legitimate income."

A local newspaper report detailed the consequences of not paying enough attention to the differences between the source of data and the provider of the data:

In defense of Dun & Bradstreet, said Paul Gray, assistant U.S. attorney assigned as prosecutor, "the investigation states that Dun and Bradstreet does not check the accuracy of the information supplied to it. It only reported the information came from [the defendant] himself.

But apparently for banks and credit rating services, the Dun & Bradstreet rating that valued [the defendant] at more than $50 million was sufficient."

Linkages

When you seek data, do not restrict your search. No only can one source provide several important types of data, but multiple sources should be checked to generate data on the same point. For example, do not rely on either on-line data bases or non-on-line sources alone for data.

To illustrate how and where data obtained from on-line data bases can be linked with data from other sources of CI, we present below a summary of the sources of information for an actual CI project prepared by a major aerospace contractor seeking information on the technological capabilities of one competitor in a particular market. That report obtained some data from each of the listed sources. The sources marked # can be accessed, in whole or substantial part, through public on-line computerized data bases.

\# Annual Reports of the Competitor

\# 10-K and Quarterly Reports of the Competitor

\# Proxy Statements of the Competitor

  Competitor's Product Brochures

  Competitor's Directories

  Competitor's Briefing Packages for Investment Analysts

\# Magazine and News Articles

\# Presentations by the Competitor's Employees at Technical and Professional Conferences

  Organizational Charts of Competitor

\# Investment Bank Reports on the Competitor's Performance and Plans

Advertisements Placed by the Competitor

\# Financial Directory Data

\# Contracts Awarded by the Federal Government

Case Studies of the Competitor from Business Schools

Interviews with Customers

Interviews with Competitors

Interviews with the Corporation's Own Management, Marketing Personnel, Program Managers, Engineers, and Scientists

Interviews with Former Employees of the Competitor

From this list, the company identified the data sources which made the most significant contributions to the noted portions of the final report as follows:

1. *Overview and History of the Competitor:* Magazine and news articles; competitor's product brochures; business school case studies

2. *Organization and Product Lines:* Financial directory data

3. *Financial Data:* Annual reports; 10-K and quarterly reports; investment bank reports

4. *Corporate Strategy:* annual report; magazine and news articles; investment bank reports

5. *Company Relationships:* interviews

6. *Marketing Strategies:* interviews; review of advertisements

7. *Research and Development Strategies:* annual report; presentations at technical conferences; interviews

8. *Defense Contracts:* Contracts awarded by the federal government

Tiering Your Research

Often you may not be able to find the exact data you need to locate quickly or easily. This is particularly a problem when you may have limited resources, in terms of time and/or funds, available to take on what turns out to be an excessively demanding project. In such cases, divide your assignment up into tiers, that is, levels of research. Attack the more general level first, seeking easily obtained data from public sources which can be reviewed quickly. Then analyze your data in terms of what it tells you about what additional, more specific data you need to complete your task, and where that may be. By doing this, you can often save both time and money, focussing your resources on locating critical bits of more specific data in the second tier.

COLLECTING DATA

Overview

The tools of CI are relatively simple. They include computerized data bases, directories, and the telephone. But most importantly they include the mind. The key is using these simple tools to find the right data. It is like the story about the nuclear reactor which was having problems. After months of trying, finally the engineers were about to give up. Someone suggested almost as a joke, calling on Dave, a retired handyman, who seemed to be able to make anything work. In despair, the engineers called Dave.

Dave said that he could fix the reactor, but that it would cost $10,000. The engineers said, ok, if you can fix it, we'll pay. Dave went to the control room, stepped up to the console, and hit it on the left side. The reactor started to work. Sheepishly the engineers said that they would need an invoice to pay Dave so much, particularly for so little work. And they got one. It read "For hitting the control console—$10. For knowing where to hit, $9,990. Total—$10,000."

As indicated above, one effective way to get started with CI research is to treat the data you are seeking like a commodity. Ascertain who might generate it, who might collect it, and who might analyze it. Only after that point should you try to figure out where such data has been placed in the public domain.

Since the most commonly used sources of raw data include the U.S. Government, state and local public records, corporate sources, the media, trade associations, and investment reports, a few words on each may be in order.

The Federal Government. Here, the key is patience and politeness. Very often, even if you have located a government office which could have the data you are seeking, or is wired into the right industry network, you still have to locate just the right person. And that can take doing. However, there is a lot there.

For example, one firm was seeking information on a competitor's current research and development efforts in an information technologies field. One solution was to identify any federal government contracts with the target firm, and then study both the specifications for the contract as well as the contractor's reports on its progress (obtainable under the Freedom of Information Act). This would tell a lot about how far the competitor's research and development had progressed.

Public Records. Now what is "public" can vary from state to state, but there is a lot of data that is available to the public. In one case, a firm was considering buying a corporation which also owned a casino, so it wanted detailed, but apparently unavailable, data on the performance of the casino. Also, to evaluate existing management, it wanted very detailed information on how every other casino in that city was doing. The solution was a call to the state casino control board which disclosed that the state kept and published monthly records of the activity of each casino, by type of game. The data was filed to let the state determine how much taxes it could expect from casinos and to assist them in regulating the casinos.

Corporate sources. Even with the movement of corporations toward going private, there is still much data public on large non-public corporations. For example, a public corporation may be spending much money to track a now-private competitor. Thus, a study of the public corporation's records and reports, as well as interviews given to industry analysts, may tell you what the public corporation sees and thus, indirectly what the private firm is doing.

Media. The media, particularly local media, can be invaluable. One firm was very interested in plant-level data on one particular factory owned by a major international petrochemical corporation. A careful survey of the trade press disclosed general information about the plant's initial and ultimate potential capacity. This was important data, but it did not indicate what the plant now produced or at what stage its expansion plans stood. But other media, and a somewhat unconventional source, were combined to produce the data. A telephone call disclosed that a local newspaper had run several stories on the plant because it was the town's largest employer. The stories included information on the current number of employees, where the latest new construction stood (with pictures), and even data on the specific products currently being produced. A call to the local Chamber of Commerce produced a four-color glossy booklet on the benefits of doing business in the area. And, featured in the booklet, was a full page spread by the plant. That full page included color photos of the plant, taken from an airplane, as well as many interior shots, showing equipment and finished products. An experienced analyst could estimate from these photos alone the size of the plant and its output. But the photos in connection with clippings from the local paper and data on the plant's expansion potential provided the detailed CI sought.

Asking the Right Question

Before you even start to gather data, you must ask the right question. You do not just ask for "some information on...." That approach dates from a time when competitive data was more difficult to get. You would not do that today any more than you would go into an IBM store and ask for "some office stuff."

One tip in making your question specific is to visualize, on a piece of paper, the report which will result from your CI. What might it say? What are its conclusions? How did you reach them? This will help you formulate where you start.

You can usually afford to start with your ideal solution, and, if necessary, compromise at a later point. Given your goal, you then work backwards to decide what kinds of data you will need to enable you to reach your conclusions. It is research turned on its head: instead of seeing what is available and working from that, you decide what you need and then look for it.

Types of Data to Be Sought

You do not often obtain or develop critical CI by obtaining one all-revealing piece of data. Rather, most worthwhile CI is the product of the assembly, comparison, and interpretation of many small and seemingly insignificant pieces of data. This means that your collection of data must sweep wide. To understand what data you need, you must focus on the reason that the data is being collected. Typically, CI is concerned with obtaining data dealing with some or all of the following:

—The identification of current and future competitors.
—The capabilities and limitations of competitors, including their intentions and deployment of corporate assets.
—The composition, strength, disposition, financial backing, training, and morale of key corporate groups, such as marketing or research and development.
—Weaknesses in the management and administration of a competitor which may impact its market performance or response time to your competitive moves.
—Development of new products, marketing techniques, or related organizational changes.
—The impact that your firm's actions, and the actions of other competitors, have had on the competitor's operations and future plans.

Of course, you may need CI on other subjects, such as those listed in Appendix C, Competitor Analysis Outline.

Locating Data—Basic Rules

To locate the raw data you may need for your CI, remember to reason out who else has an interest in that data and why they have an interest. Each person or organization you have identified in this way is a potential source for your raw data. For example, if you are interested in the sales of certain departments in chain drug stores, using these criteria could lead you to trade associations, corporate annual reports, and trade publications.

Do not limit yourself. You probably should reason that a trade publication could have an annual issue, covering major financial or marketing issues, including those in which you are interested. But do not ignore that publication's advertising department. It has its own special interest in current data about its readership in comparison with the entire industry, so it can sell advertising. As a result of this interest, some advertising departments have extensive market/sales surveys in great detail which can provide invaluable data.

Even sophisticated research can be assisted by data gathered in relatively mundane places. For example, Wall Street financial analysts have for several years been following the fortunes of defense contractors involved in the development of the Stealth bomber and other highly-classified defense programs. These programs are regarded as so sensitive that the firms involved are often not permitted to disclose that they even have the contracts nor are they permitted to disclose details of their performance under those contracts. For these reasons, these programs are often called "black" programs, to contrast them to overt, or "white" programs. Yet Wall Street financial analysts have been able to develop fairly detailed estimates of the Stealth bomber program's current status and the fortunes of defense contractors involved in it by doing the following:

—They compare the development of a "black" program with similar projects developed in "white" budgets.

—They analyze a contractor's bottom line operations. By subtracting revenues and costs associated with a firm's non-secret business, the analysts believe that they can estimate the financial impact of a secret project.

—They track company operations in an industry trade publication, *Aviation Week and Space Technology*, principally seeking unauthorized revelations about the project and the contractors.

—They use on-site techniques, including counting the cars parked outside of a factory. The presence of full parking lots is taken to mean that the program operating at the facility is accelerating. The construction of additional facilities and the presence of an unusual number of cars with government license plates or stickers is seen as confirming that conclusion.

"Soft" CI

Not all CI that you get will be "hard" data. In some cases, all that is available is "soft," that is, non-quantifiable. In others, it may be that the best CI is "soft." For example, in a story about keeping up with Japanese research and development, four scientists at the Battelle Pacific Northwest Laboratories commented as follows:

[W]e have found that scientific and technological advances in Japan are often first communicated by word of mouth within the Japanese scientific community.... It is also important to recognize that many significant technical developments in Japan do not appear directly as experimental results or as business news.... Thus technical journals and databases are helpful but only supplementary. Closer contact between our countries' specialists is the primary way to supply the necessary details and overall insights.

In other contexts, sometimes "soft" sources of data may be better and more current than "hard" sources. To take another example, in the summer of 1987, *The Philadelphia*

Inquirer was engaged in a major marketing offensive to develop increased suburban readership. A local popular magazine ran a detailed story on that campaign, including in it a copy of the map currently being used by the *Inquirer* to plot its marketing offensive.

This article not only gave information which would not be available to the competing newspapers in the area, and their out-of-state parent corporations, but it also gave a detailed case study of what is involved in conducting such a marketing effort. This could be valuable to other newspapers elsewhere in the country facing the same problem, either offensively or defensively.

Do not overlook one of the best, but often least obvious sources of CI, even "soft" CI, your competitors. Consider for example the following practical advice given to radio station managers on how to compete in selling advertising:

[C]all every TV station, newspaper, shopper [publication], billboard company, speciality [*sic*] advertising company and magazine in your market. Call the Yellow Pages representative. Set up a meeting. Ask each to bring information on his or her medium, including rates. In a short time, you will have media kits on file for all the media in town.... This kind of intelligence gathering should help you.

You may find an idea for promoting your station on another media.

You will have important information on how to counter the competition's claims and you will know what your clients are being told.

Another important source of monitoring is direct mail. It is a good idea to give stamped, self-addressed envelopes to a media buyer or key advertiser so he or she can drop information into the mail that is mailed to them. For example, a special package or station newsletter could provide you with intelligence that will help you make better decisions and set more workable strategies.

When developing CI on micro-level data, you typically must rely on identifying a stream of data, and then on capturing or even sampling that data at different points. From that, a clear picture can often be constructed or, at least, an estimate developed of what the stream itself looks like.

In some situations, however, this method does not work. This may be, for example, because there are differing types of product distribution systems involved, so that there is no single stream from which data can be drawn. Rather, you may face dealing with a limited amount of data, drawn from differing, independent sources. Usually, that type of data is non-comparable, to the extent that any data at all is even available. This problem may occur for a combination of several reasons:

—Some firms in the industry carefully avoid disclosing any data, believing that such release will not benefit them, but, at best, will serve to harm them.

—Some firms do not release data because they do not know what their own data is, so they cannot release it.

—Some firms are not interested in either providing or collecting data on certain subjects because they perceive that this data deals with, for example, markets that are either too small for them to focus on or where they perceive that they do not and will not have an important role.

One approach to filling this gap is to use a "consensus" approach. In a consensus approach, a verbal picture of the industry or of the market serves as a substitute for quantifiable data. Typically this works best when seeking to identify the largest participants in a given market. Thus, instead of obtaining sales figures, and then ranking the firms by comparing sales, you would establish a list reflecting a consensus of available data as to the rank order of the firms. This approach usually involves the following elements.

Identification of potential participants in the market using inputs, such as the following:

1. advertising materials;
2. interviews with sales representatives and retailers;
3. membership lists of trade associations which appear to be important to companies in the market;
4. trade publications or directories listing who supplies products or services to the market;
5. interviews with industry observers, including consumer groups and trade publication editors;
6. interviews with key individuals to identify additional participants, to exclude others, and to obtain a picture of the firms generally identified as the largest. Those interviewed could include:

    A. representatives of major market participants to obtain their perspectives;

    B. marketing and product personnel at firms identified as potential participants.

Collateral source materials for additional detail on potential participants and on the market, typically including:

1. articles on the industry and industry sales trends;
2. specialized publications printed for industry participants;
3. consumer interest publications;
4. annual reports and investment analyses.

SEC Reports

By now, most business planners realize that almost any analysis of a competitor whose stock is publicly traded and its plans must begin with a review of the corporation's annual report filed with the U.S. Securities and Exchange Commission (SEC). However, many stop with the annual report. The annual report should be just the beginning. There are numerous other required and optional publications which can provide even more information than that in the annual report. Consider, for example, the following descriptions:

—*Annual Report*—it must contain basic financial information, covering a period of five years, together with an identification of members of the board of directors. It may also contain a letter from the Chairman or President, discussing the past year, management's analysis of the past year, or a report on public issues of importance to the corporation's future. The level of detail in the sections not required by the SEC varies widely. Consider for example the relatively bare-bones approach of the 1986 Annual Report of Kimberly-Clark Corporation, which had five pages of general statements about the corporation's past year in the Chairman's letter and "A Profile of 1986." That featured statements at a very general level of detail such as "[third quarter s]ales and operating profit for disposable diapers improve over the first quarter." ... On the other hand, the 1986 Annual Report of Pfizer Inc. included over 20 pages of detailed discussions of the performance of specific operations, at a level of detail like this: "World-wide sales of [a specific heart medication] increased by 10% in 1986 to $509 million.... International sales of [it] increased by 17% in 1986."

—*Form 10-K*—an annual document, which may incorporate the annual report by reference. It contains detailed financial statements and information on senior management, as well as on competition, corporate assets, research and development plans, and other issues affecting the corporation's overall operations. This can be quite detailed and revealing.

—*Notice of Annual Meeting and Proxy Statement*—this is mailed out in connection with an annual meeting and in connection with any other stockholders meeting called to consider major corporate decisions, such as a merger or acquisition. For the annual meeting, it contains information on all directors, plus information on the compensation of top officers. When issued in connection with a merger or acquisition, it contains very detailed information on the proposal, together with management's recommendation for the way stockholders should vote.

—*Quarterly Reports*—Various kinds of specialized reports are required by the SEC. Some corporations distribute them with no other materials included with them. Others use the distribution of the quarterly reports as an occasion to communicate with stockholders and with the investment community. For example, Colgate-Palmolive Company's Third Quarter Report—1986 was titled *Colgate-Europe: A Regional Strategy to Build Shareholder Value.* This included four pages detailing Colgate-Palmolive's production and marketing operations and plans for its European operations.

—*Annual Meeting*—Some corporations distribute a summary of the proceedings of the annual meeting of stockholders. In addition to recording the results of votes, they may, but are not required to, summarize questions and answers from stockholders and even reprint addresses of corporate management to stockholders.

Some corporations also release other data, not required by the SEC. For example, H.J. Heinz Company has traditionally released the transcript of major presentations to security analysts, such as *Heinz In New York: Shaping Our Own Future in a World of Marketing Myths,* a 36-page brochure containing the remarks and graphic presentations by Heinz's President to the New York Society of Security Analysts in March 1986.

You should realize that some of these documents must be filed even when a corporation's stock is not traded. For example, Montgomery Ward & Company, Inc., which is a wholly-owned subsidiary of Mobil Corporation, prepares a Form 10-K for Montgomery Ward's own operations, which is filed in addition to all of Mobil's own filings. This is because Montgomery Ward has outstanding corporate debentures which are still traded on the New York Stock Exchange. So, even if a competitor has been acquired by a privately-held company or has gone private, do not assume that none of these reports are available.

ETHICS

Extreme care should be taken to avoid crossing either legal or ethical boundaries in collecting CI. There is a distinct and critical difference between industrial espionage and CI. Industrial espionage involves the breaking of the law or of contracts to collect confidential data on competitors. This can range from stealing samples at trade shows to breaking into computers.

There exists a grey area between industrial espionage and CI where actions are taken which are not illegal but which are questionable or immoral. This can include such widely disparate activities as going through a competitor's trash or interviewing a competitor's employees to gain information, while pretending to be considering them for a position with your firm.

For example, there is a very fine line to be faced in dealing with laws like the Securities and Exchange Commission's prohibition against the trading of securities using inside information. When dealing with only public documents, there is no problem. But problems may arise when that information has been checked against and enhanced through other devices such as personal interviews.

Whether through inadvertence or for a personal reason, the interviewee may well reveal information that is not public. What can happen? In one celebrated case, a major financial printer was charged with violating this law, based on allegations that employees of the firm profited by seeing information about public corporations before it was released.

But the problem of dealing with inside information is not limited to those working for the company whose stock is affected by the information. Another case involved the *Wall Street Journal* columnist R. Foster Winans. The U.S. Government charged that he had profited from inside information received by virtue of his position as a financial reporter. He was convicted, not of violating the SEC rule against insider trading, but of profiting from information received by his employer, the newspaper. He was convicted and lost his job. The ultimate implication of this case for CI research is as yet unclear. However, it seems to apply if CI research produces inside information which could affect the value of the stock of a publicly-traded company. In that case, if the person who generates this seeks to profit from it, or gives it to someone else who trades stock based on that information, then all those persons expose themselves to severe legal penalties.

REFERENCES

Albert, William M., "What's On Tap?", *Barron's,* June 18, 1984, pp. 30, 32–33.

American Institute of Certified Public Accountants, "What else can Financial Statements tell you?", 1987.

Conley, David, "Competitive Analysis Case Study A," SCIP Annual Business Meeting and Workshop, March 19, 1987.

Fried, Stephen, "Won't You Be My Neighbor?", *Philadelphia*, August 1987, pp. 81–83, 128–137. This contains a detailed analysis of the strategy and tactics currently being used by a major metropolitan newspaper in seeking to expand to suburban markets.

"Getting to the heart of Japanese R&D," *High Technology*, February 1987, p. 7.

Guyon, Janet, "Company Meetings With Analysts Raise Questions About Disclosure," *Wall Street Journal*, December 18, 1986, p. 1.

Jenkins, Holman, Jr., "How Wall Street Deciphers the Pentagon's 'Black Budget'," *Insight*, August 17, 1987, pp. 42–43.

Keiser, Barbie E., "Practical Competitor Intelligence," *Planning Review*, September/October 1987, pp. 14–18, 45. A basic overview, tying together elements of a competitor profile with likely sources for the needed CI.

Kronholm, William, "Corporate annual report may go the way of the dinosaur," Associated Press, March 16, 1987, printed in *The Morning Call*, March 16, 1987, p. B10. This story

discusses the possible demise of the "glossy report" to shareholders.

Lytle, Chris, "Attacking Newspapers," *Radio Only*, April 1986,
pp. 15–16, 18, 20.

Ethics

Derra, Skip and Ted Agres, "Competition drives market for industrial espionage," *Research & Development*, June 1987, pp. 63–
64, 66, 70.

Greene, Richard, "Never Mind R&D, How About T&G?", *Forbes*,
September 24, 1984, p. 142.

"Guard Your Garbage," *Fortune*, September 3, 1984, p. 9.

Johnson, Robert, "The Case of Marc Feith Shows Corporate Spies
Aren't Just High-Tech," *Wall Street Journal*, January 9, 1987,
pp. 1, 12. This deals with a case where an employee crossed
the line from collecting CI to committing a crime.

Miles, Gregory, "Information Thieves Are Now Corporate Enemy
No. 1," *Business Week*, May 5, 1986, pp. 120–121, 123, 125.

Poncavage, Joanna, "Paper tycoon faked credit, U.S. says," *The
Morning Call*, April 17, 1987, pp. B1, B5.

Rubin, James H., "Court upholds convictions of former *Journal*
reporter," *The Morning Call*, November 17, 1987, p. B13. A
summary of the U.S. Supreme Court's decision upholding
the conviction of a reporter from the *Wall Street Journal*
and two others for profiting from the uses of insider
information.

Sanger, David E., "I.B.M. and Hitachi in New Accord," *New York
Times*, November 12, 1986, pp. D1, D5. This outlines accom-
modations reached by several major manufacturers to settle
claims of stolen computer technology.

"Western Publications Enhance Espionage," *Insight*, August 31,
1987, p. 39.

5
Analyzing Data

IMPORTANCE OF ANALYSIS

While CI cannot be conducted without acquiring raw data, it is the analysis which converts that relatively useless raw material into usable information. The care with which the analysis is conducted is as important as the quality of the data collected. For example, those conducting the analysis must be careful not to project their own biases and preconceptions onto the data. Failure to do that can render even the best data worthless.

As a staff member of the U.S. Senate Select Committee on Intelligence put it in the context of government-level intelligence operations:

Prejudice on any question, or its milder form, conventional wisdom, whether out of bureaucratic self-interest, ignorance, habit, or intellectual bent, is death to analysis. On the other hand, fear of disaster (or its obverse, a passionate thirst for victory) can overcome decisions about the focus of analysis, compel critical examination of prejudice, and diminish the relative importance of bureaucratic self-interest.

STAGES OF ANALYSIS

Before analysis can even begin, the raw data must be collected, as discussed in detail in Chapter 4. In some cases, as the analysis proceeds, you may find that additional, supplementary data must be sought.

Following the initial acquisition of the raw data, you will be involved in a series of steps, which may often blur into each other:

1. Evaluation
2. Analysis
3. Integration
4. Interpretation

EVALUATING THE ACCURACY OF DATA

Once you have gathered data, you must not just accept that data as accurate. You must establish the probable accuracy of that data for it to have any meaning. If you don't do that, you may be analyzing a combination of very good data, marginal data, bad data, and even disinformation. Even if you can draw some sort of conclusion from that amalgam, you run a substantial risk of drawing the wrong conclusion. Once you have a sense of the accuracy of the individual pieces of data, you can then analyze it properly.

For example, if a piece of data is quite reliable, but is contradicted by a piece, the source of which is considered unreliable, you can then identify the correct data. You can also minimize the impact of or ignore entirely other, less reliable, data.

There are three principal steps in evaluating the accuracy of data:

—Identify the actual source
—Evaluate the source
—Classify the data

Identify and Evaluate the Source

You must always keep in mind the reason a particular source is supplying data. Remember, some reports and studies often take their data from other reports and studies. Be clear as to the ultimate source of data.

Example: In considering the potential impact of improved transportation on a nation's economy, the first step may be to get reliable data on that nation's GNP. In one actual case involving an underdeveloped nation, research located data from a number of U.N. sources and from a major international bank.

From each report, the source of the data was tracked backward. These sources were found to be the U.S. State Department and the European Economic Community. Additional checking disclosed that the data all ultimately came from one source within that underdeveloped country. This source was a set of newsletters put out by that nation's central bank. These were the only source of all published economic information. However, in the newsletters, the author noted that the data given was merely a rough estimate. The result was that all of the data, which looked official and appeared in "all the right places," was actually generated by one person, who would not even vouch for its accuracy.

Having determined the actual source for the data, you must now evaluate the reliability of that source so you can classify its data as to accuracy. The bases on which you judge reliability are an evaluation of the source's reason for collecting or releasing the data and a judgment of the source's historical record for accuracy.

Knowing the ultimate source of data can help you determine its accuracy. For example, data generated by a trade association lobbying for a particular bill in Congress can be assumed to advocate a point of view. Data collected and analyzed by the Census Bureau may not have this same slant. Checking for the source of data is crucial to eliminating both disinformation and false confirmations.

Disinformation. incomplete or inaccurate information designed to mislead others as to your intentions or abilities. This differs from fraud, which involves distributing erroneous or false information with an intent to mislead or to take advantage of someone relying on that information. This is covered in detail in Chapter 6.

False Confirmation. when a second source of data appears to confirm the data from a particular source, but does not actually do so. Typically, this is due to the second source having received information from the first source, or both sources having received their data from one common source.

CLASSIFYING DATA

CI is like assembling a jigsaw puzzle in that you have individual pieces of data which can appear meaningless or insignificant, but, when assembled in the proper manner, produce a picture. There are three key differences from jigsaw puzzles: first, you must get the pieces yourself; second, you may not be able to get all of the pieces; and third, you may have to remove some of the pieces because they are disinformation, not information. With the pieces you keep, you should classify them as to their probable degrees of accuracy. You may choose to develop your own system, or just to rely on hunches. But, as more data is collected and more people are involved in collecting it, you will find that you need some systematic way of marking data to identify its likely accuracy and the credibility of its source.

In Appendix B, we have set out some guidelines for a very formal classification system. This system takes into account the need to account both for the reliability of the source of the data as well as the accuracy of the data itself. The system is not designed to be applicable to all CI contexts, but rather to set out a model for the most detailed and formal approach.

DETERMINING RELIABILITY

To determine the reliability of a source of data, the original source of the data and the source from which you obtained it must both be considered. For example, current employees of a competitor may or may not be reliable sources depending on their attitudes toward their current employer as well as their perceptions of the use to which the information they are giving will be put. Data from suppliers of a competitor, even those with whom you also do business, may be influenced by the desire to please, a reluctance to discuss other clients, or a lack of perception on the part of the individual providing the data.

The past performance, when available, of individual and institutional sources of data is the best basis on which to judge reliability. A supplemental test of the reliability of the source is to consider whether, under the conditions facing the source, the source could have actually obtained the specific data within the limitations of time, access, and financing which the source faces.

DETERMINING ACCURACY

Understanding the true source of the data is the first step towards determining its accuracy. However, do not be deceived into believing that an independent or academic source of data automatically guarantees its accuracy. Use your common sense. The press has recently been reporting about the publication of incomplete or even incorrect scientific papers, as a result of the pressure on many scientists to publish on a regular basis.

ANALYZING THE RESULTS

Analyzing the results of research differs with each project because it is a function of the task, the data collected, the audience for whom it is being done, and the experience of the person doing it. In spite of the differences in each case, there are several basic rules which should be followed:

—Study how a project like this has been done before, assuming that there was one before and that it is available to you. Compare it with other data and watch for omissions. In one case, a major corporation was concerned about the strength of a competitor which operated two separate, but related businesses. The first was the consumer sector; the second the raw materials division. The consumer section seemed strong, but raw materials seemed weak. However, a close look indicated that each division had the same promotion track, and equal representation on the Board. Comparing this company with others similarly structured disclosed that this company did not price inter-company transactions on the same basis. It did it at the cost of the raw material—not at market price as competitors did. The result was that the consumer division was made to appear more profitable, and the raw material division less profitable, than they actually were.

—Make sure you know how accurate your data is.

—Identify and deal with potential disinformation.

—Structure your research results to help you conduct your analysis.

—Don't make assumptions—find out. In one case, a multinational corporation was preparing for a major structural change in manufacturing operations. At the last minute, someone asked about its ability to compete with its largest competitor. The answer was that the two companies would end up using the same internal structure. However, fortunately, someone questioned the "known" fact. It turned out that the competitor was highly decentralized, just the opposite of what it appeared to the public.

—Review your results to assure completeness and consistency.

—Look for important omissions and anomalies.

—Decide if further research is warranted. If so, design it using your results as a starting point.

—Be imaginative and be alert to the importance of detail.

—Separate your data from your conclusions.

Some people use the word A–I–D as a help to remind them how to conduct an analysis.

Anomalies. Look for anomalies, data which does not seem right. The existence of an anomaly may indicate that your assumptions are wrong, or that there is more going on than you might realize.

Indicia. Look for direct indications of what you are seeking. For example, in a high-technology business, is your competitor hiring more researchers, building more new facilities, being awarded more patents, or devoting more funds to R&D than in the past?

Displacement (or *Disaggregation*). If you cannot find out about the aspects of a business in which you are interested, step back and look at the entire operation. Then eliminate all data dealing with areas in which you have no interest. What is left may be indistinct, but it shows you the outlines of what you seek. For example, if you cannot determine what a competitor is spending on new research facilities, find out its total financial picture, and then eliminate expenditures for non-research facilities. What is left sets the outer bounds of its expenditures in research. In one case, CI research located a Ph.D. thesis which had been written based on data which was not public. The data was aggregated to conceal company-specific information. But other data had also been published, by a U.S. Government department, but aggregated in a different manner. By studying each, and using other sources of specific data, estimates of company-level data were able to be generated. The puzzle was a little like the problem of the seven men in a room, where the admiral is drinking scotch, his brother-in-law is left-handed, and the man with the bow tie arrived last. Given this assortment of clues, you have to decide which one killed the reporter. But, just as with that puzzle, this one could be taken apart with a combination of creativity and sheer effort.

In addition, be careful that you understand exactly what has been said and what has not. Increasingly, many businesses use their own vernacular, a kind of private language. Sometimes, this is designed to provide clarity and accuracy to those who use data. In other cases, it is designed to keep outsiders from understanding what is actually going on or even to affirmatively create desired impressions in targeted groups.

For example, in the area of food marketing, certain phrases have fixed meanings and others do not. Compare "lean" with "lite" or "no preservatives added" with "organic." The first two in each set have specified legal meanings; the second do not. Under U.S. Department of Agriculture rules, "lean" meat or poultry cannot possess more than 10 percent fat by weight. In contrast, "lite" has no such fixed meaning. Generally, products labeled as "lite" have fewer calories or fat than some other (perhaps unspecified) product. On the other hand, it can just mean that the product is light in taste or in color. "No preservatives added" means that there are no synthetic preservatives in the product. But the product can still contain artificial coloring. Also, this label can be used on products which never had preservatives added. In comparison, the Food and Drug Administration considers "organic" as undefinable. A label "organic" on food does not necessarily mean that the food is free of chemical fertilizers and pesticides, although some states cooperate with farmers to certify foods grown this way.

Also make sure that you understand the origin, nature and way in which any statistics you obtain have been collected and manipulated. Through both error and choice, numbers do not always reflect reality. As the Director of the Census Bureau has noted,

The reasons for statistical abuse range from ignorance to arrogance. Sharing the blame is the 'give me any numbers you have' mentality of some statistics users who are willing to sacrifice accuracy for immediacy. When quality is questionable, however, any numbers are not superior to no numbers.

REFERENCES

Codevilla, Angelo, "Comparative Historical Experience of Doctrine and Organization," in Roy Godson (ed.), *Intelligence Requirements for the 1980's: Analysis and Estimates*, Washington, D.C.: National Strategy Information Center, Inc., 1980, pp. 11–36.

"Degree Revoked," *Insight*, April 6, 1987, p. 60.

Holmes, John, "Cure Sought For Doctored Research," *Insight*, March 23, 1987, pp. 56–57.

Lovelock, Christopher H., "Conducting and Interpreting A Marketing Research Study," Harvard Business School Note 9-582-152, Cambridge: HBS Case Services, 1982. A good overview of the steps typically involved in developing a marketing research project and interpreting its findings.

Keane, John G., "Questionable Statistics," *American Demographics*, June 1985, pp. 19–21, 48. A readable analysis of some of the most common mistakes and distortions in presenting statistics.

Phillips, Richard, "Guess What's Cooking For Dinner?", *The Chicago Tribune*, reprinted in *The Morning Call*, November 9, 1986, pp. G1–G2.

"Push To Publish Research Linked To Mistakes," *The Morning Call*, January 15, 1987, p. A10.

6
Disinformation

WHAT IS DISINFORMATION?

Because CI involves converting your data into a cohesive picture of a competitor, you must be aware of business disinformation. But, being aware of it is not enough. You must develop tools to identify and to handle it.

Disinformation's meaning can be seen in the word itself—it is something that looks like information, but it is not information. The word itself comes from the world of intelligence and international politics, where disinformation encompasses both fraud and forgery. As the text of a secret U.S. Government document on disinformation (released to the press from an unknown source) reportedly says, disinformation "combines real and illusory events... with the basic goal of making (the target) THINK" what the initiator wanted. According to this document, among the objectives of a disinformation plan is to keep the target "preoccupied" and "off balance."

Disinformation in the business world is not as extensive as it is in politics and espionage, for it falls short of fraud. It is more akin to a magician's illusion:

a classic misdirection...to present [the target] with an array of evidence and allow him to draw his own conclusions. If we show him the proper evidence, he'll reach the conclusions we want him to. If we simply show him a finished product, he's sure to question it closely, but if we show him our preparations, he'll make his own decisions.

TYPES OF BUSINESS DISINFORMATION

Active and Passive Business Disinformation

Active business disinformation intentionally misleads people with erroneous or exaggerated information. Passive business disinformation involves concealing relevant information. In each case, business disinformation is aimed at establishing false value judgments, creating erroneous impressions, diverting attention from defects or problems, or hiding facts.

Purposeful Business Disinformation

Business disinformation usually originates from the business itself. For example, a firm may have an officer give an interview to a local newspaper, with an eye toward improving the firm's community image. During the interview, the reporter's expected questions about the firm, its plans, and its future are answered, sometimes with great care, by the subject of the interview.

The reporter leaves with notes, quotes, handouts, and impressions. When the article is prepared, all of these go into the final product. In producing the article, the conclusions drawn by the reporter may not be precisely correct. In fact, the person giving the interview may have worked quite hard to help the reporter draw certain conclusions without ever having stated them as facts.

If the conclusions are not harmful to the firm, the firm usually has little incentive to seek a correction. In fact, even if a correction were requested and eventually given, from the point of view of business disinformation, damage has been done. Retractions and corrections, even when entered in some public on-line data bases, rarely catch up with those who read the original story.

Once printed, the article often becomes an important input to the "trades" (trade publications and newsletters), to investment analysts, and to others following the firm or the industry. In turn, these sources may generate a second level of disinformation, based on the first level of disinformation but less able to be identified with it.

Accidental Business Disinformation

Business disinformation can also arise inadvertently. For example, due to the rise in interstate bank mergers, many small regional banks have been reviewing their long-range plans to see if they should seek to be acquired, prepare to oppose an acquisition, or seek to make defensive acquisitions themselves. As part of this review, they often hire outside consultants to advise them on their options.

In one case, a bank holding company (BHC) retained such a firm. The BHC did not intend to publicize this action. The firm was hired to provide general advice; this was not the first step in either an acquisition or a sale program.

However, the firm which the BHC hired did not "get the message" about avoiding publicity. In fact, the advisor sent a press release about its being hired by the BHC. This was done because the advisor was seeking to publicize its hiring in order to get additional business. The press release was printed by the business media, disclosing that the advisor had been retained by the BHC and noting that its role was to advise the BHC as to its options.

Some who saw the resulting article came to the erroneous conclusion that this BHC was actively seeking to be acquired, assuming that the BHC had arranged for the publicity. Why else, they concluded, would the BHC release this information, particularly in publications serving areas served by none of the BHC's subsidiaries.

The result was that for the next several months, the BHC was misidentified as a potential acquisition target. As a result of the undesired attention, the BHC had to take steps to protect itself against a possible takeover while deciding whether or not it should even actively seek a takeover.

WHY IS BUSINESS DISINFORMATION CREATED?

Misleading the Competition

Sometimes, business disinformation is generated specifically to mislead competitors. For example, in many industries, the development of new products and processes is costly and time-consuming. If you believe that a competitor is ahead of you in a particular area, you may abandon your firm's work in that area, since you cannot ever catch up.

One way to determine the technological status of competitors has been the routine use of on-line data bases to identify their new patents as they are issued and new products as they are released around the world. In some industries, reportedly including pharmaceuticals and electronics, this practice has been met by a counter-measure—conscious business disinformation. Some companies purportedly patent "mistakes" to throw their competitors off the track. Others make product announcements "rife with false information," seeking to lay claims to markets before their technical or sales forces can actually produce the product.

Making the Company Look Good

In some cases, business disinformation is generated to make the sourcing company look good. It has as one of its effects the misdirection of competitors, but is typically designed to accomplish other objectives as well. For example, a manufacturing firm was planning to expand its production capacity by building more plants. To accomplish this, it sought out joint venture partners, and was well launched on this course. However, it was going to take time to put all of these facilities in place. In addition, the firm found that some potential participants were willing to make only the vaguest commitments, expecting to commit to the actual investments after they saw the firm's progress on other fronts.

The company sought to gain time for its expansion plans to take hold by keeping out potential competitors until its new capacity was on-line. It also wished to project a very positive image of its strength and progress to assure its current investors and joint venturers as well as to entice additional ones. The result of these efforts was business disinformation. It was produced by granting interviews and arranging for stories on new production capacity which overstated the status of new projects, either in terms of availability for new production or of its likelihood of going forward.

To competitors, the firm made itself seem stronger than it really was to keep others out of its market. To potential investors, the firm appeared to be strong and getting stronger, thus hopefully generating a band wagon effect. So long as the company did not engage in fraud, such as misrepresenting the status of these projects on its books in a material way, this was not illegal. It was business disinformation.

Misdirecting Insiders

Business disinformation can also be found in situations involving a firm's own employees. For example, if in early

1986 you had been studying the London daily newspaper industry, you should have located extensive data showing high labor costs, in part due to prevailing trade union practices. You probably would have assumed that these costs would not decline significantly in the short run. However, your CI research should have disclosed that a major force in that market, Rupert Murdoch, owner of the *Times of London* and other major publications, had recently built a highly automated printing plant outside of London, with the announced goal of using it to start a new afternoon daily newspaper.

In retrospect, it seems that the announcement was business disinformation. Following a 1986 strike, Murdoch quickly moved all of his London-based newspapers to this new facility and fired all union strikers, with the aim of breaking the back of the trade unions to lower wage rates and eliminate restrictive job practices. Many observers now believe that the facility had been set up for just this eventuality. The announcement of another future purpose for this facility was business disinformation. For, even if that facility was intended to provide a home for a newspaper, that was not its only or even its primary function. Observers were misled by assuming that a specific statement on the facility's intended purpose was a complete one.

SPOTTING POTENTIAL BUSINESS DISINFORMATION

What contemporaneous clues were there that the Murdoch announcement might be business disinformation?

—After construction started on the new plant, Murdoch opened negotiations with the unions on acceptance of computer technology, such as that planned for the new plant, in newspaper operations. These negotiations broke down.

—The new facility has a high degree of security built-in, including eight-foot-high walls and surveillance cameras. These features were considered quite desirable when Murdoch faced threats of industrial violence after relocating his newspaper operations.

—There are no indications that U.S. suppliers of the automated equipment to be installed there announced that they had received a contract for such a major project. This might have indicated that those building the plant wanted to minimize any discussion about the plant's potential capacity or scope of operations.

—The location of the new facility put it outside of the area traditionally within the jurisdiction of the printers' unions which already represented workers at the *London Times*. In the United Kingdom, this could have served to discourage unionization activity at the facility.

—At his other, non-United Kingdom papers, Murdoch has utilized state-of-the-art technology in press operations in all operations.

—Murdoch, a man who has been described as acting "audaciously" in the past, reportedly has made no secret of his "frustration" with the printers' union practices since entering the British Press industry.

None of this data was secret. Yet most analysts did not look for data which undercut the announcement about this facility's purpose, because they were not looking for disinformation. If they had, they would have isolated this additional data, and included it in an analysis of the future of the British Press, particularly of Murdoch's operations. In turn, this could have caused an analyst to at least question the conclusion that feather-bedding practices of trade unions would continue to cripple the operations of the British daily press, particularly those of Murdoch's operations.

HANDLING POTENTIAL BUSINESS DISINFORMATION

Being aware that disinformation exists and seeking to determine whether your competitor is using it is like an examination for cancer:

—If you don't look to see if it is present, and it is there, it can be destructive. You may not recognize its destructive effect until it is too late to counteract it.

—If you look for it, you may not spot it, even if it is present. In that case, known as a false negative, your CI analysis will be tainted by the disinformation in a direction and to a degree which you cannot appreciate.

—You may find what you think is disinformation, when it is not really there. In that case, known as a false positive, you will simply be more suspicious about the credibility you assign to what is really accurate data, and more reluctant to rely on it without further confirmation.

—You may be correct in spotting it. In that case, handling it properly will permit you to avoid its damaging effect on your business's planning and marketing operations.

If you have identified data which appears to be disinformation, treat it as follows:

—If there is any question about data you have obtained, it is better to treat it as disinformation. Your doubts may be due to the lack of a traceable source for the data, your inability to confirm or to contradict it, or just because it does not feel right, such as that it is an anomalous event.

—Note whether the reason for your characterization is because of the source of the data or the nature of the data itself. If the reason is a question about the source of the data, this should help lead you to seek other sources to check on the data and away from those which might provide no assistance at best, or false confirmation at worst. If your concern is due to the nature of the data itself, then you do not have to be concerned about seeking other sources for data; you should be seeking confirmation or contradiction for data from all sources, including the original source.

—Seek alternative sources of direct or indirect data to confirm or discredit the potential disinformation. Be particularly sensitive to the danger of false confirmation, that is, relying on something else that also relied on the disinformation.

—If you are not sure whether or not the data is disinformation, try to estimate the likelihood of its accuracy and then assign a probability of accuracy to the data. This may allow you to use it even if there is a question as to its validity.

—Analyze why the potential disinformation was created or permitted to continue. If you cannot determine why the firm probably would have created it or permitted it to exist, it may not be disinformation. On the other hand, if you can deduce why it was created or permitted to continue, you may not only have identified disinformation, but you may know what the firm was trying to accomplish. This can be important in determining this firm's strategy and methods of operation. It may also help reveal the actual facts. If you know what isn't true, you may be able to determine what is true.

—Do not overreact. Disinformation may be as common in some business' contexts as puffing in the sale of cars or other consumer goods. Remember, every business wants to put on a good face. It is up to you to be sensitive to the distinction between a good image and disinformation.

REFERENCES

Barlay, Stephen, *The Secrets Business*, Thomas Y. Crowell Co.: New York, 1973. Mr. Barlay outlines the 1970s case of Player's No. 6, a cigarette marketing campaign that featured the launch of a dummy new cigarette which was withdrawn as soon as the real new product was introduced.

Ercoland, Patrick, "Fabrication Is In Fashion," *The Baltimore Evening Sun*, reprinted in *The Morning Call*, July 28, 1987, p. D3.

Johnson, Haynes, "The New Morality: Cheating To Win," *50 Plus*, December 1986, pp. 68–71. An analysis of some of the factors that have led to cheating and deception in business and government.

"Revolution on Fleet Street," *Time*, March 3, 1986, pp. 52, 55.

Safire, William, "Disinformation Preparatory School," *The Morning Call*, October 26, 1986, p. F9. This column features a dissection of political disinformation.

Stevenson, Howard H., "Resource Assessment: Identifying Corporate Strengths and Weaknesses," in William D. Guth (ed.), *Handbook of Business Strategy*, Boston: Warren, Gorham & Lamont, 1985.

Vella, Carolyn M. and John J. McGonagle, Jr., "Competitive Intelligence," *Information Times*, August 1987, pp. 5–6.

Woodward, Bob, "U.S. reportedly deceived Gadhafi," *Washington Post*, reprinted in *The Morning Call*, October 2, 1986, p. A26.

7

Integrating CI into Business Plans and Planning

Integrating CI into your business planning requires that the CI you seek has a direct relevance both to the planning process and its objectives. In defining the CI you need, you are also refining the business planning process. Similarly, when you define the objectives of your business plan, you are, in part, establishing the inputs needed for that plan from reliable CI.

In this chapter and in the two that follow, we deal with the intimate relationship between CI and specific elements of business planning. This chapter deals with those instances where CI can be directly integrated with business planning as it is now conducted. Chapter 8 deals with CI practices which can be integrated into ongoing business planning activities, or which can be added as additional elements. Chapter 9 discusses shadowing markets, a process which can be added to a business planning function, and Chapter 10 discusses defensive CI, a consideration which business planners should take seriously.

CI FOR SPECIFIC LEVELS OF PLANS

To demonstrate where CI fits into existing business planning efforts, we use one of the classifications discussed in Chapters 2 and 3; the distinctions among planning at the corporate, line of business, and functional levels.

In planning at the corporate level, CI should be used to develop the following information which is vital for the establishment of a competitive strategy for each industry in which the corporation is involved:

—Projections of future market size and rates of growth for each industry.

—The cost structure of each industry, trends in key cost components, and technological threats and opportunities.

—The nature of competition in each industry, including:

  1. the intensity of the competition;
  2. the dominant firms;
  3. the dominant firms' share of the market;
  4. potential new competitors;
  5. barriers to entry to the market, and;
  6. competitors' perceptions of the competitive nature of each market.

In planning at the line of business level, CI should be used to develop the following information which is vital for the establishment of a competitive strategy and the making of tactical decisions for each line of business:

—Relative market share of the firm. (To know this, you must know the size of the total market.)

—Comparative quality of the firm's product or service. (To determine this, you must already know who are its competitors and what are their competitive products and services.)

—Perception of relative quality among existing and potential customers.

—Strengths of current and potential competitors. (This requires a determination of who potential competitors are, and why they are potential, not yet actual competitors.)

—Recent personnel changes in key positions or recent purchases of new equipment or facilities by competitors.

—Shadow market planning. (This is covered in Chapter 9.)

In planning at the functional level, CI should be used to develop the following information which is vital for the making of tactical decisions:

—Technological developments by competitors.

—Probable direction of competitors' research and development efforts and likely short-term impact of these developments.

—Overall financial strengths of competitors as well as their relative financial strengths.

—Likely changes in the regulatory environment affecting both your firm as well as its direct competitors.

—Shadow market plans. (This is covered in Chapter 9.)

CI FITTED INTO EXISTING PLANNING STEPS

If we approach the structure of business planning in terms of the specific steps discussed in Chapters 2 and 3, CI can fit into existing business planning efforts at a number of specific levels.

Identifying Opportunities

Use CI to identify and evaluate actual and potential competitors, to measure the market, and to determine the perceptions held about your own company's strengths and weaknesses.

For example, businesses need adequate CI to plan what to do even before they consider entering a market. Examples of where CI should have been used are numerous. In one instance, a German firm, Natterman & Cie GmbH, purchased a Pennsylvania-based pharmaceutical company. The goal of the purchase was to make the United States-based firm serve as a means of marketing Natterman's all-natural line of pharmaceuticals. Evidently Natterman believed that the United States was a logical market for all-natural pharmaceuticals, given the evident national focus on health and natural substances. However, Natterman sold the firm after three years when it concluded that its products were not compatible with the United States market. Use of CI before the acquisition might have disclosed that the national concern with all-natural substances does not always translate into buying decisions, particularly when there is a price differential. Put more bluntly, when it comes to "all natural," Americans do not always put their money where their mouths are.

Selecting Objectives

Use CI to determine what objectives your competitors have established. If your competitors have different objectives from your own, you should not anticipate that they will behave as you would when facing new competitive scenarios. Also, knowing what their objectives are may help you to develop new objectives which permit you to take advantage of some areas which are not critical to your competitor. In fact, if your strategic objectives differ enough from those of a competitor, it may indicate that that firm is effectively no longer a direct competitor.

Establishing the Business Context

Use CI to develop hard data about the business and regulatory environment you are in or will enter. This may include developing shadow market plans of your key competitors as well as determining the present and future regulatory and financial environments facing both you and your competitors. Having established the business context for your competitors, you may be able to develop a competitive scenario to assist in preparing your own plans. A competitive scenario is an analysis of what one or more competitors can be expected to do in response to changes in market and other conditions affecting the activities of each company. The analysis is based on a profile of the competitor, including estimations of its intentions and capabilities, derived from a study of its past actions, and of the perceptions, style, and behavior of its current and future management. Each competitor's expected actions are measured against the same set of expected market conditions and changes.

Putting this in the context of the luggage industry may help to illustrate this. Each year, a trade publication, *Travelware*, releases a survey of manufacturers in which they have identified their best-selling product for the previous year and where they identify what they expect will be their best seller for the current year. Before using this, remember to apply the rules outlined earlier, because you cannot just accept this survey on its face. For example, ask yourself whether the firms are likely to be frank in identifying the best-selling product for the prior year. They probably were, since this can be informally verified by those at the retail end. However, do not immediately assume that the projection of the best seller for the current year is as accurate. A firm may have reasons for identifying a product as a major seller when it does not expect it to be a significant market participant. For example, it may seek to mislead competitors about its intentions to move in or out of a higher-priced market. Also, firms are not always accurate in their predictions, even if they are truthful. To confirm that, you could compare the prior year's predictions with the announced results. You may find that firms vary widely in their ability to predict their own markets. Make sure that you are not misled by their errors.

Identifying Options

Use CI to check on the track record of competitors. If they have tried and rejected an option you are considering, determine why have they done so. That may save you from making the same mistake and allow you to proceed without incurring the same costs as your competitor did when failing.

Evaluating the Plan's Progress

Use CI to obtain data on competitive responses to your activities and to keep abreast of changes in conditions which may cause you to change your own plans. By obtaining this on an ongoing basis, you can noticeably improve your ability to respond to changes in both the business environment by modifying the plan as well as by making those corrections necessary to keep the plan on track.

CI AND EXISTING PLANNING SYSTEMS

Applying yet another common distinction among plans, that is between strategic and tactical plans, we see where CI can fit into current plans and planning efforts.

Strategic Plans

In developing strategic plans, among the key considerations are the following:

—Anticipate and assess uncontrollable socioeconomic factors which impact the business. To do this, you must determine what these factors are, such as energy prices, or trade barriers, and then identify their importance to your plans. CI should be used to identify the historical variations which these factors have faced and evaluate potential future fluctuations.

For example, A.D. Dasler KG, the German manufacturer of Adidas athletic footwear, decided to make its footwear in the United States. There were reportedly at least two reasons for this decision. First, Dasler felt that a foreign label would find it difficult to compete with American-made products for consumer acceptance. Second, Dasler felt that establishing a plant in the United States would permit them to overcome existing trade barriers to the import of athletic footwear. However, Dasler has now seen U.S. trade barriers lowered, so that it is facing severe competition from non-United States makers of athletic footwear. Apparently no one noted the likelihood that the current Administration in Washington would not support trade barriers and would in fact lower them if possible. Also, Dasler was evidently not made sensitive to the fact that, in many markets, Americans prefer foreign-made goods to American-made products. Here also, preliminary CI could have helped avoid these competitive problems.

—Determine profit margins in various segments of the businesses in which the corporation operates as well as the past and expected future growth rates for each, and their relative stages in product/ service life cycles. This would be utilized in one or more of the popular matrix analyses of business units. CI should be used to determine this data for the industries of interest. Unfortunately, efforts are made to analyze a business under one of these matrix systems without even knowing what the industry base line data shows.

—Determine probable competitor responses to potential competitive strategies. This is particularly important in dealing with industries where one or two firms dominate lines of business. Using CI can help to evaluate potential competitor responses so that you can better take advantage of them. For example, a CI analysis may show that the largest firm in a particular market is unlikely, based on its track record, to retaliate for competitive moves which do not threaten its total sales, as distinguished from its market share. Thus, an appropriate strategy could involve efforts to capture new business while leaving existing business alone in an effort to avoid provoking a sudden and costly response.

Marketing Plans

Marketing plans, in contrast to strategic plans, tend to require micro-level data instead of macro-level data, and generally need current rather than historical data. For example, marketing planning generally requires some of the following to be effective:

—The identity of a firm's competitors. While it may seem astounding, many firms, particularly in the services fields, do not actually know the identity of their current competitors. This should be among the first CI assignments.

—Relative market share and total market size, as well as overall market trends. CI should be the source for this, instead of just accepting the prior year's estimates plus some anecdotal trade data. The better the data here, the better able a firm is to evaluate its true position in the current market.

—Analysis of each major competitor's market position and economic strength. When CI provides such data, it can be invaluable. For example, knowing that the major participant in a market is financially weak in other, unrelated businesses, may give the opportunity to undertake a strong assault on a previously sacrosanct market. That is because the CI disclosed that the dominant competitor is not financially able to respond to an assault, thereby improving the likelihood that such an assault will succeed.

—An evaluation of the likelihood of indirect competition from other products or services. Too often, as discussed in Chapter 3, businesses may not see potential competition coming. Engaging in ongoing CI monitoring of markets, firms, and technologies may be an effective way to avoid costly and potentially damaging new entries to existing markets.

—Technological trends and competitors' responses to them. Here, effective and current CI may serve as an early warning system for marketing departments. Tracking a competitor's research and development efforts, for example, may be the best, and perhaps the only, way that you become aware of a major new product before its introduction is announced.

IDENTIFYING NEEDED CI

Regardless of the type of business planning you are engaged in, when you need CI, you should use the following list of questions as a guide to help you establish exactly what CI you need:

What CI do you think you need and why do you need that specific CI?

Can you restate your CI requirements as one or more questions to be answered?

Can you focus these questions? That is, can you shift from a general question, such as "What are my competitors' marketing plans?" to "Is a specific competitor preparing to introduce any new industrial products in the next six months?"

How important and valuable would the answer to that question be? This should tell you how much effort and resources should be devoted to answering it, and how specifically it must be answered.

Will you need this data on an ongoing basis or just once?

When do you need this CI? The time-frame within which you have to operate may prevent you from pursuing valuable, but time-consuming, avenues.

What kind of data will permit you to develop a response to your question? For example, do you need direct evidence of your competitor's intentions, such as an announcement of the hiring of a new advertising agency to handle selling the product? Alternatively, will indirect evidence suffice, such as reports in regional business publications of promotions which may be related to marketing a new, but unknown, product?

Do you need macro-level data or micro-level data? Will it have to be current or historical, or both?

What data do you already have on this subject? This should force you into an exploration of previously unutilized or underutilized internal resources. These can include interviews with employees who have attended trade shows, or with sales personnel who can provide feedback from customers and from non-customers as well.

Is additional data available? If so, where? If not, what kind of data will be an adequate substitute, given your constraints?

DISSEMINATION

In What Form?

The final step in any CI process is dissemination. For CI to be used, whether in planning or in other contexts, it must be given to those who need it, in a suitable form, and in a timely manner.

Dissemination may be direct or indirect. For example, if a request is made for a CI report on a potential acquisition target by the director of new business development, security and other considerations may require that the CI report be given directly to that person and only to that person. On the other hand, a CI report on a shadow market plan of a key competitor may be given to several individuals, such as the director of planning and a marketing manager. Each, in turn, may redistribute part or all of the CI, or integrate the CI into reports or projects with which they are involved.

CI may be communicated orally, in writing, or in graphics form. While the most common form of communication is the written report, the most effective means of dissemination may involve using a combination of these means at once so that those receiving the CI are more likely to retain and understand the CI.

An oral presentation is fast, and permits CI to be given to a large number of consumers at once. However, it has the important disadvantage that miscommunications can occur more easily with this than with either form. Another disadvantage of an oral presentation is that usually there is no permanent record that the CI was provided to the consumer, nor of what that CI was. The lack of any record may hinder both the person seeking to use the CI, who may need to refer back to some element of the presentation, and the presenter, who does not have any exact record of what was said, so that he or she can build upon that CI in the future.

Written presentations are slower to make than are oral ones, if for no other reason than it takes longer to write something than to say it. However, once it is written, CI does not change its content when it is transmitted from one consumer to another. This is not true with oral presentations. Also, written presentations can be reproduced and sent to many consumers in a short time. Using electronic means, such as the electronic mailbox, finished CI can be sent to a number of consumers virtually instantaneously. However, remember, the wider the distribution of written CI, the more likely it is that this CI will be available to persons or even organizations for whom it was never intended. For more on the subject of defending against CI, see Chapter 10.

The use of graphics in CI presentations can be quite effective. In fact, by using graphic aids, such as charts or illustrations, you can enhance the effectiveness of an oral presentation in several ways:

You can emphasize critical points or concepts;

You can make it easier to understand complex numeric comparisons; and

You can give those at the presentation something to take with them, a copy of the graphics, without having to distribute the full text of the presentation.

Which method or methods you select depends on the need for clarity, accuracy, speed, and security. While an oral presentation may be quick to prepare and present, it may be difficult to have the consumers grasp complex financial relationships merely by hearing a recitation of data. While a graphic presentation can help clarify comparisons of data, preparing complete and understandable graphics may require more time than is available. In CI, as in many other areas of business, timeliness determines whether or not information is useful. Precise information which arrives late may be less desirable than a rough approximation which is available on schedule.

Making the Case

The form of presentation is, in part, determined by the need for the CI report to be useful and persuasive to the consumers. In presenting the results of a CI report, analysts should avoid two common problems, in addition to those detailed in Chapters 5 and 6:

"Group think," that is, the pressure among members of a group working on a project to find a common denominator and reach a consensus instead of stressing diversity, if applicable. "Because judgments by consensus are the lowest common denominator, they are often of poor quality. Truth is not necessarily found in the middle of the road, nor is it a statistical average."

The "Sherwin Williams mentality" (from the advertising slogan, "We Cover The World"), that is, providing analysis on every conceivable aspect of a topic, whether the consumers have specifically asked for such CI or not.

Avoiding these and other traps can raise the CI analyst's credibility in the eyes of its consumers. As a former member of the CIA has put it in the context of national intelligence:

Intelligence is in essence a guessing game, albeit one that is grounded in fact, logic, and experience. It can be a useful tool to the policy-maker, but it is not, even in its purest form, a magic art.

However, past successes, just as past failures, can have an impact on how CI reports are regarded. For example, as one observer has noted, "[t]he more successful an intelligence organization becomes, the less are its reports questioned and the greater the chance that it will fail."

Integration by Participation

Xerox Corporation has had a corporate intelligence function for 20 years. It has evolved in many ways since then. For example, in the area of design and technology planning, that system now operates as follows:

CI is focussed on specific functions or processes that firms, whether or not competitors, do "extremely well." For example, Xerox has "learned a great deal about material distribution from retailer L.L. Bean."

CI is no longer "just the job of those specifically assigned to the task." For example, "the people responsible for making [product] improvements gather intelligence as well."

CI's most valuable tools are visiting trade shows, reading periodicals, and "watching how competitors do business." For example, each year Xerox personnel from many disciplines visit Japan and other countries and produce a study on their findings.

CI can involve reverse engineering of competitive products which are "attractive from a manufacturing or design standpoint." Such products are acquired, torn down, and made available to engineers. In turn, they evaluate any patented technology which Xerox may be "up against." Also, they study those non-patentable features as well as the applied engineering and manufacturing principles that reduce costs and improve quality.

CI disclosed that Xerox was spending twice as long as a top competitor in getting a product to market, using twice as much labor, and spending three times as much on tooling. These disclosures "led to some fundamental changes in product design, production, and delivery."

As can be seen, at Xerox, CI is closely integrated into both planning and product development, in no small measure by having employees in those areas involved in a part of the CI process.

REFERENCES

"4th Annual Best Sellers/Best Bets," *Travelware*, March 1987, pp. 25–29.

Garvin, Andrew and Hubert Bermont, *How to Win with Information or Lose Without It*, Washington, D.C.: Bermont Books, 1980. A short primer on the importance of good information for business managers, stressing a hands-on approach.

Giza, Richard H., "The Problems of the Intelligence Consumer," in Roy Godson (ed.), *Intelligence Requirements for the 1980's: Analysis and Estimates*, Washington, D.C.: National Strategy Information Center, Inc., 1980, pp. 189–206.

Marchetti, Victor and John D. Marks, *The CIA and the Cult of Intelligence*, New York: Dell Publishing Co., Inc., 1975.

Prescott, John E., "A Process for Applying Analytic Models in Competitive Analysis," in William R. King and David T. Cleland (eds.), *Strategic Planning and Management Handbook*, New York: Van Nostrand Reinhold Co., 1986, pp. 222–250.

Reinhard, Katherine, "Foreign ties to L.V. firms get stronger," *The Morning Call*, February 22, 1987, pp. B13–14.

8

Supplementing Business Planning with CI

In this chapter, we discuss two specific techniques which can be usefully applied to supplement existing business planning activities. These are reverse engineering, and benchmarking. They are only possible when there is effective CI.

REVERSE ENGINEERING

The classic definition of reverse engineering is to purchase and then dismantle a product to identify how it was designed and constructed.

This is done so that costs and quality can be estimated. In the case of non-patentable processes and devices, it can provide information on how to produce a competitive or substitute product. In the case of patentable products, it can educate engineers on how the patented process works, and enable them to avoid patent infringements in designing their own competitive products.

This technique can provide engineering "cues." For example, it may indicate ways to pack and ship items at a lower cost. It may show that there are less costly ways to accomplish similar ends, either in terms of the cost of raw materials or in terms of the manufacturing techniques used. Also, the same analyses may provide important marketing clues. For example, reverse engineering may indicate that a competitor's products are exceedingly costly to make. This in turn may mean that the competitor's profit margin is lower than anticipated. In turn, marketing can use this CI to help it develop a new marketing campaign, designed to price its product below the competitor's cost of manufacturing, but above its own manufacturing cost. This could eventually force the competitor to completely withdraw from the market in question.

However, reverse engineering can deliver even more CI. For example, one firm found that by routinely buying products produced by a competitor, it could tell at what capacity the competitor's factory was operating. They found out that each product from a particular plant was given a unique, and consecutive serial number. In addition, the firm found that output from the key plant was routinely distributed through one distribution center. A little CI soon identified a store from which the item could be purchased which carried little inventory. Therefore, buying a new item there each month was like taking a sample from the factory's output stream. Comparing serial numbers over time gave the firm the ability to estimate how many units the factory was producing each month.

Reverse engineering often serves to convince one's own personnel that a particular innovation is possible. As one GM official has put it, "It's pretty difficult for an engineer to argue that something can't be done, if you can bring him down here and show him that it is already in production."

In addition, the techniques of reverse engineering may even be applied to services as well. Of course, technically this is not reverse engineering, since there is nothing which has already been engineered, but it has been given that name.

In this context, marketing professionals and financial experts would replace the engineers. Working with a CI professional, they would obtain data on the service in question and then "tear it down" to its basics.

For example, if a firm is competing in the financial services industry, it could obtain copies of a competitor's annuity contracts from a state insurance department, where they are filed as a matter of public record. To get rates, it could consult its own agents, review industry data books, or just call someone selling the product, and get a quotation. Information on supportive marketing efforts, such as national television advertising, may be obtainable from a publication such as *Advertising Age*. Finally, it would obtain information on commissions paid in connection with sales, most easily from its own agents selling both product lines. Then, the company's actuaries would determine how much each element of coverage would cost. The marketing personnel would determine the loading required to cover commissions and current levels of marketing support. The cost would be compared with the pricing, and a determination made of the probable minimum levels of sales needed to support the product profitably.

At this point, the company is able to compare its own products with those of the competitor, adjusting for product differences, to determine relative competitive strengths. Also, marketing personnel could, at this point, sample consumer satisfaction with the product, adding an additional element to the "reverse engineering."

The end result is a profile of a competitive service, an insurance product, accounting for its costs and profitability. In turn, this would permit effective marketing decisions to be made in terms of introducing an identical or substitute product, or even in terms of competing in this market segment at all.

BENCHMARKING

Benchmarking is a cost analysis technique which is similar to reverse engineering. It is a process for comparing one company's operations against other firms both in and out of the market. Typically, the comparison is made with those firms believed to exhibit the most efficient operations.

This can be used at almost any level, from the product level to overall corporate operations. For example, a firm may use benchmarking in the same way that it would use reverse engineering. That is, it would focus on a particular product and determine all of the elements which went into establishing the costs of production.

In benchmarking, as distinguished from reverse engineering, the focus is on comparison. Thus, to analyze how to most effectively compete head to head with a particular product, a firm might determine both its own and its competitors' manufacturing and distribution costs, taking into account such matters as both the cost and yield of raw materials, as well as the number of manhours and hourly rates involved. The goal is to determine where you have a relative advantage, and then to exploit it.

Continuing on this example, suppose a benchmarking comparison discloses that while your hourly rate for labor is lower, you need more hours of labor in each item, so that your total labor costs are higher, per unit. Your solution might be to increase productivity rather than to seek to transfer production to a labor pool with lower hourly rates. Similarly, benchmarking might also disclose that while your competitor is not as efficient in the amount of materials it uses in a product, it has an advantage over you because it pays less per unit of material than you do. Here, one indicated solution might be to seek a better price on the material. Another may be to switch to another less costly material with which your evident engineering and manufacturing efficiencies permit you to avoid increased manufacturing costs with the new material.

Benchmarking is also used to analyze a firm's own efficiencies by measuring its performance against a number of different firms. For example, a firm may compare its direct mailing operations with those of a direct mailer in an entirely different business, to determine if its own overhead is reasonable. One reported instance of this involved Xerox's study of its own order processing with that of L.L. Bean, a leading mail order clothing company. Similarly, it might compare its bookkeeping operations with a retailer or a bank's billing departments. Here, by enabling the firm to collect detailed data on specific operations, CI can enable a firm to undergo a rigorous self-examination.

Of course, it might be unrealistic to assume that your firm can ever be as efficient as the best departments in a variety of firms in different industries. But by looking beyond your own industry, you will avoid an insularity which has been the cause of the downfall of many businesses.

A form of benchmarking can also be used in comparing your firm's standards of operation with those of its competitors. In this case, the goal is not to determine the most efficient cost levels of each component of an activity. Instead, it is a process to permit you to compare your performance with that of another firm.

For example, in one case, a firm was concerned about the productivity of its sales force, as compared with that of the sales force of a major competitor. It chose to approach this problem by benchmarking its own operations against both the major competitor and sales operations of a highly efficient manufacturer of similar, but not competing equipment.

The firm found that its sales representative costs, as a percent of revenues, were competitive. However, the analysis disclosed that the outside firm paid substantial commissions in comparison with those in its own industry. However, that same firm seemed to receive better levels of productivity from its sales representatives. Dissecting the sales management system through benchmarking disclosed that the firm with the higher commission rates was focussing attention on new accounts, and used formal new account quotas.

This benchmarking brought on a review and eventual restructuring of the sales management and marketing program. The sales force was divided so that certain sales representatives focussed only on new accounts, and others serviced existing accounts. Commission rates were increased. The result was increased productivity, and an improved market share.

Without effective CI to provide the detailed information needed for this benchmarking, it would not have been possible. What would have occurred would have been a generalized study, focussing on internal information only. CI provided a window on the world allowing new information and a new perspective to be introduced.

REFERENCES

Blumenthal, Philip L. Jr., "Financial Model Preparation," Technical Consulting Practice Aid 2, New York: American Institute of Certified Public Accountants, 1983. A practical guide to this area.

Finein, Edward S., "Why it pays to go sleuthing," *Design News*, December 1, 1986. A candid interview with Xerox Corporation's Chief Engineer and Manager of Competitive Practices and the Product Delivery Process for the Reprographic Group.

Furey, Timothy R., "Benchmarking: The Key to Developing Competitive Advantage in Mature Markets," *Planning Review*, September/October 1987, pp. 30–32.

Handel, Michael, "Avoiding Political and Technological Surprise in the 1980's," in Roy Godson (ed.), *Intelligence Requirements for the 1980's: Analysis and Estimates*, Washington, D.C.: National Strategy Information Center, Inc., 1980, pp. 85–111.

Markowitz, Zane N., "Hidden Sector Competitor Analysis," *Planning Review*, September/October 1987, pp. 20–24, 46.

Palmer, Joseph E., "Financial Ratio Analysis," Technical Consult-

ing Practice Aid 3, New York: American Institute of Certified
Public Accountants, 1983.

Risen, James, "GM 'spy center' dissects competition," *The Los
Angeles Times*, reprinted in *The Morning Call*, December 6,
1987, pp. D1, D3.

Schmid, Robert E. Jr., "Reverse Engineering a Service Product,"
Planning Review, September/October 1987, pp. 33–35.

9

Enhancing Business Planning by Shadowing Markets

As indicated in Chapters 7 and 8, CI has numerous specific direct applications in all types of business planning. In addition, due to the growth of data on which CI can operate as well as due to an increasing sensitivity to the capabilities of CI, a new application is developing for CI; that of shadowing specific markets. Shadowing markets, made up of shadow market planning and the development of shadow market plans, can be an effective additional element in business planning, particularly in marketing-oriented planning.

WHAT IS SHADOWING MARKETS?

"Shadowing markets" is a term the origin of which is not as clear as it might seem at first glance. It appears to indicate only a surveillance of markets. To a limited degree, this is true. However, the concept is broader, tracing its origins to the British political concept of the "shadow cabinet."

A shadow cabinet is made up of members of the party out of power in the Parliament. Each member of the shadow cabinet is assigned a government department to follow. It is that shadow cabinet member's responsibility to do the following:

—Keep track of all policy and personnel changes in the target department.

—Assist the party not in power in developing its own policies in response to policy initiatives of the government or even in advance of those initiatives.

—Be prepared to assume the direction of the target department should the government change.

—Serve as a resource for the party out of power by being able to anticipate policy and personnel changes in the target department before they occur. In a sense the shadow cabinet has become a model of the government's department.

Shadowing markets can take one of two different forms, which are sometimes carried on at the same time, and by the same people:

—Preparing a shadow market plan. This is a one-time assignment, the end product of which is a document which is as close to the competitor's market plan as CI can make it. The goal would be to duplicate that document, if there is one, or to put down on paper what the competitor's plans are likely to be.

—Engaging in shadow market planning. This involves tracking all of the elements which go into the competitor's marketing and market planning. Depending on the industry and the competitor, this can include regular monitoring of personnel changes, new corporate acquisitions and divestitures, emerging financial constraints due to the performance of unrelated divisions, and other objective and subjective inputs which the competitor receives for its planning and implementation processes. The goal is to enable one or two persons to act as if they were the competitor and to be able to respond to "what if" competitive questions.

Both of these require monitoring competitors, at a level of detail which will come as a surprise to most planners. Since you cannot usually find data about the plan itself, you must immerse yourself in that competitor, its philosophy, operations, and even its history. To do this, you do not have to get direct access to the competitor's internal documents and plans. Much can be learned from a study of external items and data, even about the most confidential subjects.

As Daniel Ford, who researched U.S. ability to respond to a Soviet nuclear attack and determined what our plans are in this most secret of all military areas said:

[I]t is unnecessary to get access to the planning documents themselves to gain an insight into how and when Pentagon plans call for U.S. leaders to push the button.... Form, the biologists say, follows function.... How individual weapons are all put together with other equipment will be further evidence of the general strategy that has been adopted.

CI can help you shadow competitors. For example, just by using an on-line data base such as PTS MARS, you can track announcements of new marketing campaigns, the hiring of new marketing and advertising firms, and the appointment of new marketing personnel for many businesses. By itself, this data may be valuable. But CI uses it as an input to produce a shadow market plan or to engage in shadow market planning.

Of course, it is easier to develop a shadow market plan if there is direct data on your competitor's intentions. It is not impossible to get that data. For example, suppose that you are interested in the activities and plans of ALPO Pet Foods, Inc. a subsidiary of a major United Kingdom marketing firm.

One way of getting data for this type of CI would be to use on-line data bases to monitor the trades, the financial papers and magazines covering this portion of the consumer products. However, applying CI techniques, one of which is to treat data as a product, might lead in other, more profitable directions. For example, viewing data as a commodity means you ask who makes it their business to track ALPO? Your response could include stock analysts (interested in the fate of its current owner, Grand Metropolitan, PLC). However, there are at least three other potentially more useful sources of data which are often overlooked. One would be a local business publication, and the other would be a major local paper. Both of these sources are available through on-line data bases. The third is the company itself.

What kind of data can such sources provide for shadow markets? As an example, the local newspaper serving ALPO's headquarters, *The Morning Call* of Allentown, Pennsylvania, regularly runs stories about ALPO and such things as its executive changes. From ALPO, you might have obtained a copy of its 1986 history (which you would have spotted referred to in local business publications, on-line). That document noted, almost in passing, that while the company adopted the current name in 1983 to provide greater identification with its pet food operations, this was also done "to separate the pet food operation from other business activities." Also, the company's former name "has been retained as a viable corporate identification for new business opportunities into which the company is expanding." These comments should enable you to put into context announcements about diversification and observations that the company was not seeking additional pet food acquisitions.

The Shadow Market Plan

A shadow market plan is a document which is designed to be as close as possible to a competitor's market plan. Shadow market planning can be undertaken whether or not your competitor has a marketing plan of his own.

To develop a shadow market plan, you obtain data about a competitor and try to construct a competitive scenario, a picture of what your competitor is probably doing. Based on that, you then estimate what that competitor will be doing over the next several years under certain sets of facts.

From the point of view of the business seeking to develop and use a shadow market plan, it is probably most useful to have its form and presentation track the form and presentation of similar documents used by the business developing the shadow market plan. The goal is not actually to reproduce your competitor's document, assuming there is one, but to restate the competitor's plans and capabilities as the competitor actually sees them. To make sense of them, you may have to have them restated in terms or using concepts with which your company is comfortable, rather than in concepts and terms used by the competitor.

In preparing a shadow market plan, some firms add an additional element which may not be present in the original: an evaluation of how the targeted competitor perceives the business preparing the shadow market plan. Doing this is quite difficult, as it requires concentrated analysis of the competitor's people and how they think. In addition, the results may tend to be more sketchy than are other aspects of the shadow market plan. However, they can be extremely useful.

Firms seeking this additional perspective would do well to consider having outsiders prepare this portion, for the results often are startling and unpleasant. For example, is a staff employee of Ajax Corporation going to feel comfortable in telling his or her superiors that the competitor, Consolidated Inc., does not regard Ajax as a serious competitor or that Consolidated believes that Ajax is poorly managed, with an excessive focus on short-term results? Potentially disturbing news may be better delivered by an outsider. It is also more likely to have a receptive audience.

The kinds of data needed for developing a shadow market plan are similar to those required for shadow market planning. Some examples are included in the section on shadow market planning below.

Shadow Market Planning

A shadow market plan differs from shadow market planning in that the former is a project-oriented operation and the latter is a process. The dividing line is not a hard one. For instance, one can produce shadow market plans while engaged in shadow market planning.

In its purest form, shadow market planning requires that one or two persons would, for most purposes, "become" the competitor being followed. Their role can be likened to the role of aggressor squadrons in most air forces. These squadrons are made up of top pilots, operating equipment as similar as possible to that which a potential adversary would use. These pilots are then trained to think and respond in the same way that the adversary's own pilots would, using their preferred tactics and subject to their command limitations. The goal is to provide an opponent for pilots which duplicates, as much as possible, the way the adversary's pilots and equipment would respond in combat and other situations.

Interestingly enough, the most common non-military application of this technique is found in football. There some teams have players learn to duplicate the "look" of an opponent's offense or defense, so that the first team and coaches can practice "against" that opponent before a game.

In business, shadow market planning requires the same dedication as is found in aggressor squadrons or in football. The person or persons who will be monitoring the competitor must, in a very real sense, become the competitor. To do this, they must become familiar not only with financial statements, but with virtually everything involving that competitor on a regular, perhaps even daily basis. The scope of this can be broad. Typically it includes, but is not limited to, the following:

—Monitoring personnel changes affecting the operations of areas of your particular interest as well as in other, non-related areas. This requires finding out about these people, perhaps from local papers.

—Reviewing the full text of press releases and speeches, not just the stories in the trade press.

—Attending trade shows to meet with competitor personnel and contractors, such as ad agencies. In this way, data can be gathered and a competitor's personnel can be evaluated.

—Reading corporate documents ranging from new technical product brochures to company newsletters.

—Following technological developments by tracking professional society papers, and technical articles by key research personnel.

—Learning about the background and track records of key executives.

—Debriefing new employees who have had contact with the competitor. These may be either those who have worked for the competitor in the past or have observed the competitor from another angle, such as from the perspective of a trade association.

—Tracking regulatory matters in which the competitor is involved, such as licensing matters or consumer protection enforcement actions.

—Debriefing those with current contact with the competitor, such as salespeople who have lost sales to the competitor, employees who work with employees of the competitor on industry and other committees, dealers who carry a competitor's products in addition to your own, marketing specialists for an evaluation of the capabilities of the competitor's new advertising agency, etc.

—Studying the competitor's track record and prior history, to understand where its personnel came from and what has been their experience.

The result should be that the person or persons involved in this process can think as the competitor thinks. Not only should they be able to provide current information on what is or has been, but they should be able to provide a valuable and fairly accurate estimate of what will happen.

Curiously, to perform the last function effectively, that is to be able to anticipate how a competitor may act or react, it may be necessary to make sure that those involved in this process are not contaminated by their own employer's preconceptions. Just because their employer would not respond in a certain way should never influence the evaluation of a competitor's potential response. As has been observed in the context of analyzing competitive marketing strategies,

Although there is clearly no certainty that the competitor would in fact respond as you would if you were in his or her place, it is generally a reasonable expectation that rational managers will respond in similar ways to a given situation. If one's competitors have in the past acted in what at least seemed to be an irrational manner, such a pattern must of course, be taken into account. In many cases, *what seems to be irrational competitive behavior may, however, simply suggest that one does not really understand his or her competitor's situation.*

CASE STUDY

An example of how these concepts are applied will help in understanding their importance. Assume that the CI assignment is to determine the shadow market plans of a major insurance company, which we will call Mega Insurance. In addition, those involved are charged with tracking key developments, particularly as they deal with insurance sold to businesses, the "commercial lines," in the Mid-Atlantic area.

The potential sources for raw data are vast and varied. In part, they are determined largely by the scope and depth of the CI desired, and in part, they are determined by the nature of the target. In this case, they range from insurance industry publications to filings by Mega Insurance with the SEC. However, they should also include trade publications in industries to which Mega markets its products as well as Mega's own press releases, particularly when those press releases have not been reprinted in full text. These resources would include regional business publications throughout the

U.S., as well as newspapers serving the city where Mega is headquartered. Additional resources include on-line financial and marketing analyses of Mega's performance by securities analysts, reports in computer industry publications detailing new facilities being installed by Mega, interviews in local business publications with key personnel which may disclose future regional expansion plans, as well as public records of entities such as industrial development authorities, providing financing for new offices for Mega.

Using these resources might disclose, for example, that Mega is planning to introduce a new commercial lines insurance policy, initially in Ohio. Also, the data may indicate that Mega has contracted to build a regional office in New Jersey, and that it has recently hired a senior executive from a competitor who may be assigned to work out of that new office.

CI may also disclose the current distribution and sales of the new commercial lines product, as well as its target audience, for many companies disclose these facts to potential customers as well as to insurance agents and brokers as part of a new marketing effort. CI could also reveal the scheduled opening date, nature and size of the new facility, as well as the background and track record of the new executive.

After evaluating and confirming the accuracy of the data and its sources, this could then be combined with other information about Mega's past actions and its current attitude towards the area in question, the Mid-Atlantic states. These additional inputs could include data developed on Mega's overall corporate strategy and past record, such as whether or not it regards its commercial lines as more important than its personal lines, and also data about the economic and business development trends in the target area.

The result might be a conclusion that Mega is planning a major campaign to develop certain kinds of commercial accounts in the Mid-Atlantic area, perhaps stressing a regionalized marketing approach, coordinated from the new facility by the new executive, relying on the new commercial lines product as its cornerstone.

Once the shadow market plan has been developed, the same resources, as well as others, can be called on to track Mega's progress with its plan. For example, you might want to arrange to monitor new policies and rates filed by Mega for use in the Mid-Atlantic states by checking with the state insurance departments in each target state. Also, you may wish to monitor advertisements placed in business publications aimed at the businesses you believe are being targeted by Mega to confirm that the campaign is underway.

What is ironic here is that businesses still make little use of this technique. They do not even see where it is now used in business. But it is there.

For example, every year the National Football League, a multibillion dollar business, holds its annual draft of players. Preparing for this is an example of shadowing in action. Before the NFL draft, many teams conduct a Shadow Draft to determine what their competitors will probably do in the upcoming draft. That in turn will help determine what they will draft, and whether they will trade players for draft choices, or vice versa. In business terms, the draft and associated trades are a critical factor in determining how the team will do in the upcoming seasons. It's as if a company is making its new product, capital expenditure, personnel, and marketing decisions all in one day, knowing that they are stuck with them for the entire year.

USING INSIDERS VERSUS OUTSIDERS

The role of CI is to provide the needed information which will serve as a key, though not the only element in decision-making. Thus, those providing CI must avoid having any preconceived position either for or against any specific corporate policy which may bear on their research.

The reason for drawing a line between CI and policy is the need to keep CI unbiased and free from the appearance of special pleading. For example, if CI provided by a marketing unit stresses the need for additional retail outlets, the conclusion, whether or not valid, may be regarded as special pleading.

However, this separation between CI and policymaking must not impede effective corporate planning and policymaking. It is appropriate for CI to examine the probable effects of alternative corporate policies, particularly when this entails a determination of the way in which a particular competitor may respond. Such assessments may be made under varying, but clearly stated assumptions of potential corporate actions. In addition, the division between policy and CI must not be so rigid that CI is prevented from assessing fairly the impacts of policy decisions already taken.

These considerations may be even more sensitive in shadowing markets. In shadowing markets, firms may use either insider personnel or outside CI specialists. When a firm is engaged in shadow market planning, it might be more cost-effective for the firm to internalize that function. First, as an ongoing operation, the costs of doing it internally may be lower than the costs of contracting it out. Second, by its very nature, the firm may wish to be able to call upon its surrogate competitors at any time so that they can answer "what-if" questions. Third, it is easier to control internal personnel in terms of working for competitors, by the use of employment contracts, than it is to control outside contractors and the contractors' personnel.

On the other hand, it is often preferable to use an outside source to develop a shadow market plan. First, you do not have to train your staff for a project which, in all likelihood, they may not be equipped to do. By going outside, you are buying the training. Second, you may wish to limit the number of persons who know about the creation of such a document. Third, the shadow market plan may present conclusions about the probable actions of a competitor at odds with your firm's conventional wisdom. It is easier for an outsider to be responsible for this disclosure than it is for an insider.

REFERENCES

ALPO Pet Foods, Inc., "A History," 1986.

"Competitive Analysis," Harvard Business School Case 9-576-158, Cambridge: HBS Case Services, 1976.

Ford, Daniel, *The Button*, New York: Simon & Schuster, 1985.

Hyatt, Joshua, "Cat Fight," *Inc.*, November 1986, pp. 82–86. This article contains a rare acknowledgement of the use of shadow market planning based on an "aggressive intelligence network."

Vella, Carolyn M. and John J. McGonagle, Jr., "Shadowing Markets: A New Competitive Intelligence Technique," *Planning Review*, September/October 1987, pp. 36–38.

10

Defensive CI and Defending Against CI

WHAT IS DEFENSIVE CI?

Business persons involved with CI have gradually become more aware of the benefits of CI in areas such as seeking out and evaluating potential merger and acquisition (M&A) targets. This can be considered as an offensive use of CI. However, CI can also be applied defensively.

The difference between the offensive and the defensive use of CI is subtle yet critical. For example, using CI offensively might entail tracking the activities of potential M&A targets on a regular basis. It could also involve developing profiles of their current activities as well as activity in a specific market of particular interest to you. If your firm is already a participant in the market, that means checking on your relative position as a part of this effort, even though that effort is not aimed at your own firm.

In contrast, defensive CI involves monitoring and evaluating your own business' activities as your competitors and others perceive them. The difference is critical. This is not an evaluation of what your firm can do or is doing. Rather, it involves developing data on how others see your business, even if their perception of your business is wrong. Because it is not as focussed as more traditional, or offensive CI, defensive CI usually involves the collection of larger amounts of less focussed data than is usually the case with offensive CI. However, it still requires following the same steps and standards set out in Appendices A and C.

Defensive CI is not the same as, and should not be confused with, employee security countermeasures. Countermeasures can range from efforts to reduce theft by employees to retaining a security firm to find the source of confidential data which is being leaked to competitors. Defensive CI is more properly considered an internal countermeasure, even if it does involve protecting, or defending, against competitors obtaining data on you. In fact, conducting defensive CI may be one of the missions of an internal CI unit, as discussed in Appendix D.

Some examples of where defensive CI might have made an important difference may illustrate the scope and utility of defensive CI:

—*The Self-Fulfilling Prophecy.* In one situation, a Fortune 500 corporation found out from the newspapers that it had been profiled as a prime potential takeover candidate by a Wall Street investment firm, in part because it was reluctant to sell off several of its operating divisions. The corporation became aware of this published report about itself only after it had been published in a business newspaper. By the time the corporation found out about the analysis, substantial blocks of the corporation's stock had already been acquired by speculators. The corporation was forced into a rapid and relatively unplanned restructuring. It began a sell-off of some operating divisions to prevent the completion of what threatened to become a self-fulfilling prophecy, its takeover by outsiders.

—*The Inadvertent Courtship.* The following example, used in Chapter 6 as an example of accidental disinformation, is also appropriate. A regional bank holding company (BHC) hired an investment advisor to help it evaluate both its options, particularly as they related to expansion and acquisitions. One option was to enter into an aggressive M&A program; another was to seek to be acquired; and a third was to erect defenses against any potential hostile takeover. The investment advisor, unknown to the bank holding company, publicized its retention and the general nature of its assignment. The result was the BHC quickly became viewed as a potential takeover candidate. In fact, the bank holding company had not made any decisions about takeover offers. However, in the period following the announcement, the bank holding company received numerous propositions about being taken over. As a result, the bank holding company was forced to decide more quickly than it anticipated whether or not to accept one of these overtures.

—*The Unplanned Announcement.* A major natural resources corporation acquired U.S. rights to an important new process developed in Scandinavia. Before the U.S. corporation had even acquired a tradename for the process, stories on the new process appeared in a major national news magazine, and on both network and cable television reports. The U.S. corporation felt compelled to make a public announcement about the process well before the product which it would produce would even come on the market. The corporation's reluctance to make the announcement probably stemmed from the expected loss of future advertising impact. This was because it had to announce the process without being able to coordinate that announcement with a well-prepared marketing campaign.

In each case, defensive CI could have prevented the businesses from being surprised, and could have minimized, if not eliminated, the consequences of that surprise:

—In the first case, monitoring the reports and recommendations of investment bankers through on-line resources such as INVES-

TEXT might have disclosed the takeover warning sooner and avoided the self-fulfilling prophecy.

—In the second case, regular monitoring of regional business papers as well as of industry trade publications through on-line resources such as PTS PROMT should have turned up the unexpected announcement and prevented the inadvertent courtship.

—In the third case, monitoring announcements made by the Scandinavian firm after the licensing agreement was signed, through resources such as on-line *Financial Times of London*, might have disclosed that the licensing firm was making unexpected announcements about its new U.S. licensee. Knowing that, the U.S. corporation could have avoided its unplanned announcement by contacting the licensing firm, or at least preparing for the time when it would have to respond to media reports.

As these examples show, defensive CI can pay dividends. Some firms are unwilling, however, to devote the same levels of skill and amounts of work toward defensive CI as they routinely devote to the more traditional offensive CI. This is a mistake. Your competitors may already be devoting substantial resources and high levels of skill towards developing CI on your firm.

To be safe, you should credit your potential adversaries with being at least as efficient as you are in gathering CI. Thus, you should use your own CI skills and resources to monitor information about your own business just as you monitor that of your competitors. That means going to the same external sources, checking the same on-line data bases, with the same regularity as you apply to your offensive CI work. It also means using the same analytical techniques even if that produces information surprising to your business or even unwanted by senior management.

For example, do you read your firm's external communications in the same way that competitors do? Read, carefully and dispassionately, a few press releases, speeches, and papers given by top executives to those outside the company.

Some businesses are advised to improve their image and generate new business by preparing and distributing company newsletters to those outside the company. If your company does this, read these also. To make them successful, companies are advised to include "solid information for distributors, customers, and investors" on subjects such as new sales campaigns, new products, and future advertising strategies. You may be surprised at the amount and kind of useful data that philosophy can disclose to a diligent competitor.

DEFENDING AGAINST CI

Defending against CI from a competitor is not strictly a part of defensive CI. This is because the operational details involved, principally controlling the unauthorized release of valuable data to competitors, differs from external tracking of what competitors and others are saying about you. Thus, it may be properly considered as a part of internal security. However, its goal is the same. That is to avoid being surprised by a competitor which has developed better CI about you than you anticipated.

Some firms make extensive use of trade shows, conferences, and other meetings as primary sources of raw data for their own CI. They advocate attending these meetings because they are seen as resources for gaining data from the attendees as well as from the presentations. This is, of course, proper and legitimate. Attending meetings, making and participating in presentations, and listening at discussions can and should be used to increase your knowledge about the industry and its players. And, of course, critical information may slip out which a clever competitor, like you, can pick up on to its advantage.

However, there are techniques used in connection with such shows, such as registrations under false names or without accurately identifying employers, which have caused concern in many quarters. In fact, due to such questionable techniques, some professionals have come away from conferences, shows, and trade meetings believing that future attendance at them should be strictly limited or even eliminated. They advocate this because key personnel not only may inadvertently disclose critical information, but these personnel may actually be pumped for information. Those pumping them for information use a variety of questionable tactics, including the following:

—*The Phantom Interview.* Here a potential employer, one of your competitors, talks with your key personnel under the guise of filling an empty position which does not even exist. The goal is to obtain information on your business through your employee's understandable efforts to explain what he or she does in the best possible light.

—*The False Flag Job Seeker.* This is almost the reverse of the Phantom Interview. In this situation, a trusted employee of a competitor approaches you and appears to seek employment. The goal is to use the employment and interview process to learn about your firm. The goal may even be to elicit a visit to a facility of particular interest. The employee has no real interest in any job change. He or she will use the opportunity to develop data for your competitor's CI.

—*The Seduction.* Here one of your own employees is encouraged to talk about how important or technically proficient he or she is—by flattery. The means of flattering the employee are almost limitless. They can include discussing a third-party's products, indicating confusion over a new technical development, or even challenging a professional's knowledge. The goal is to elicit the disclosure of key data about your business.

—*The Non-Sale Sale.* Here a competitor talks with those at a distance from you—such as your distributors, vendors, or licensees. These firms are led to believe they are being courted to carry your competitor's line of goods or services. This may be true, but if so, there is an additional, hidden agenda. In fact, they are being pumped for hard information on such topics as your pricing and service.

These unethical tactics have and will continue to cause many to question the value of attending trade conferences and technical meetings. But, the benefits of attending these meetings, discussed below, far outweigh the risks of disclosing critical information to competitors, particularly if you take a few simple precautions.

Benefits of Attending Meetings

Among the key benefits of attending meetings such as trade shows, trade association meetings, industry seminars, and training sessions are the opportunities to do the following:

—*Punch the Ticket.* Membership and participation in professional and trade associations is one way many of those in the private sector can "punch their ticket," that is keep in force their professional credentials. This applies not only to individuals in the sciences and the law, but to most businesses as well. Membership and participation by its employees in a trade or professional association tends to help the firm identify itself as being at the cutting edge in an area. This, in turn, may make it easier to keep key employees, to recruit new employees, and to keep credibility with its customers.

—*Show the Flag.* For many businesses, sending its employees to meetings, whether of an industry or trade group or a management training seminar, is a way of demonstrating the active role that firm intends to take in the field in question. Being an active member of an association serves to identify that business as a major participant in that line of business. This is particularly critical if the firm is new to that area or is being challenged by new entrants to the field.

—*Make the Pitch.* It should never be forgotten that almost any meet-ing, even if not strictly a trade show, can serve as a forum for a firm to develop existing business and to add new clients. Trade shows openly have this as their prime purpose. But others may have this as a secondary objective, particularly those featuring an opportunity for "networking." In still others, merely associating with participants permits selling activity, even if it is of a very indirect sort.

—*Keep in Touch.* The very reason that some firms unethically exploit meetings, the fact that they are a prime source of CI, makes them a benefit for the ethical firm as well. By associating with those active or seeking to become active in a trade or a field, you are in close touch with trends, often before they become evident in trade publications. People attend meetings to learn, to teach, to sell, to buy, and to exchange ideas. Participating in each of these functions lets you keep on top of an industry or business. In fact, some businesses have found that a good way to bring along new employees is to send them to a meeting or show and let them move around and learn. It is a little like learning to swim by being thrown into the pool. It may be difficult, but it can produce quick results.

Do not avoid industry and technical meetings because of a fear that your competitors can turn the meeting into an espionage campaign. You must avoid a fortress mentality. The benefits of attending are substantial, and following a few simple rules should prevent major damage. Remember, in many cases, failing to attend does not prevent your competitors from accumulating information about your business as much as it may cut you off from information about them.

Tips for Safe Meeting Attendance

To be able to benefit from meetings while feeling comfortable about limiting the amount of CI which can be developed about your firm, consider the following tips. (Also, these same principles apply when you or your employees are dealing with outsiders in other contexts, such as over the telephone.)

The key message here is: emphasize common sense. For many employees, merely alerting them to the dangers of disclosing critical, confidential information is enough. For others, you should consider outlining the tactics they may face and suggest appropriate responses and standards of behavior. Among the major points which should be covered are the following:

1. Executives and supervisors should not disclose anything to employees that they do not want competitors to know about without at least warning the employees about it. For example, several years ago, it was reported that an employee of a major express package company accidently disclosed the company's plans to expand to Europe. The disclosure came during a discussion at a training meeting attended by representatives of major competitors. These plans had not been made public.

2. Do not take any sensitive materials with you, even to work on in your hotel room. These materials could end up in a stack of materials in the wrong room, or they could be accidently distributed, destroyed, or duplicated.

3. If your executives or employees have contracts or work rules dealing with trade secrets or non-competition, or have a code of conduct dealing with avoiding the disclosure of confidential business information, remind them of this. You are not trying to scare them, but only to make them more sensitive.

4. Check in advance what will be given out at the conference or meeting by your firm and its employees. If possible, have someone not in the department involved with preparing and distributing the materials check them. For example, materials such as media kits may disclose or hint at data which people in Research and Development, for example, do not want in the public domain. But you must be realistic. If the investment community can determine who is building the Stealth Bomber and how much it costs, a science magazine can produce sketches of it based on known technology, and a model company can produce a kit to build a model Stealth Bomber. You cannot hope to keep everything from leaking, but you can try to control it.

5. Brief key employees on what to say about critical issues. Do you want certain things disclosed? Remember, your competitors may be doing the same thing. But be careful about what you tell your employees to say—disinformation is one thing; fraud is something else.

Warn your employees about the existence of the traps discussed above and give them some guidance on how to deal
with them, such as the following:

—*The Phantom Interview.* If an employee suspects this ploy, he or
she may be able to smoke it out, without losing the chance for a
legitimate position, by asking intelligent questions such as: Who
is the supervisor? Do you have a copy of the job description?
What sort of work would be involved? Who is doing the job now?
Why is the position vacant, or being added? Typically the
answers to these will be evasive if the interview is just a ploy for
gathering CI.

—*The False Flag Job Seeker.* First, remember, any person interviewing with you is not bound to protect your trade secrets because
they do not work for you. Be careful if the interview seems to be
directed to discussions about the future position and the work
you are doing now and will be doing in the future, and away
from the individual and the individual's experience and qualifications. Be aware if the interviewee's questions shift from those
about the position to specific questions about other areas of the
firm's activities. Watch out for indications that a facility visit is
being sought. For highly sensitive positions, you may even want
to consider preparing a non-disclosure agreement covering
information disclosed in the interview process. This is similar to
the agreement often involved in mergers where one firm agrees
to keep in confidence any information it obtains during an
inspection of the takeover candidate if the deal falls through.

—*The Seduction.* Here, warn employees to use their common sense.
Remind them that very few people are really that interested in
exactly what they do for a living.

—*The Non-Sale Sale.* Little can be done with outsiders such as those
involved in this ploy except to warn the ones with which you
have the closest relationships that such disclosures may hurt
their favored position. For example, if they disclose a special
discount they are receiving, a competitor of yours may price his
services or product so that your customer's competitor will get a
lower price. Also, it may be possible to turn these approaches to
your advantage. If these contacts can tell you what your competi-

tor was trying to find out, you may be able to figure out your competitor's next move.

Caution your personnel about the dangers of talking too freely with people with no identified affiliation or whose affiliation is with an unknown firm. That may be a blind, or that person may be there "working the meeting" for a competitor.

Tell your personnel to let you know if the competition may have learned something by accident. But do not punish someone for an accidental slip. The first time that you do that will mark the last time that an employee discloses such an accident. If you do not know about the mistake, you have given your competitor an important advantage. But, if you do know about it, you can at least try to determine why it happened, how to counteract it, and how to prevent it in the future.

Have your employees listen critically and report back. What they tell you about a competitor's CI efforts may, in turn, indicate what your competitors know or do not know about you.

You can get the word out to your employees in one or all of the following ways:

—A formal company policy statement, in the form of a memo or addition to an existing policy manual.

—An addition to a written list of company standards of behavior. Remember, these lists are usually given out at the time an employee is hired. If that is your situation, do not forget to inform all of your current employees as well of changes and updates.

—A one-time briefing of all employees or a regular briefing of all attendees before each major conference, meeting, and trade show. This can be done by immediate supervisors. However, if your firm has someone in a department such as employee relations and development who handles meetings and conferences, it can be done by them. Do not forget to find some way to brief new employees if you rely on the one-time briefing.

—Modified routine written materials distributed in connection with meeting and travel, such as expense record-keeping packages, or instructions on entertaining to include at least a cautionary message about exercising care with confidential company information.

However, do not let concern about what your competitors know or may learn about you become overwhelming. Above all, don't be paranoid. Remember, half of what your competitors think they have learned about you is wrong—and vice versa.

REFERENCES

Ascher, Amalie Adler, " 'Embalmed' plants will stand tall," *The Baltimore Sun*, reprinted in *The Morning Call*, May 31, 1987, p. G5.

Barnes, Douglass M. and Roger W. Kapp, "Strength and Strategy in a Proxy Contest," *Directors & Boards*, Summer 1985, pp. 19–25.

Kovach, Jeffery, "Spies On The Payroll," *Industry Week*, May 13, 1985, pp. 75–77. An overview of the use of outside security personnel to find unlawful or "disloyal" employee conduct.

Kovach, Jeffery, "Competitive Intelligence," *Industry Week*, November 12, 1984, pp. 50–53.

"Put Your Company in the Headlines with a Newsletter," *Top Line*, Winter 1987, pp. 4–5.

Appendix A
The CI Process—An Outline

I. Establishing CI Needs

—Identify targets; that is, specific competitors or designated lines of business

—Determine your information needs; for example, information to develop a shadow market plan

—Establish the recipients of the finished CI

—Set relative priorities among assignments

—Decide on the time frame for reporting

—Provide feedback to other stages in the process

—Review and revise CI needs in light of results, changes in operations, and feedback from other stages in the process

II. Collecting the Data

—Identify likely sources for raw data

—Develop search strategies and techniques

—Obtain data on a regular basis and/or obtain data for a one-time project

—Provide feedback to other stages in the process

—Review and revise data collection processes in light of results, changes in operations, and feedback from other stages in the process

III. Evaluating the Data

—Establish the reliability of source of data

—Estimate the accuracy of data

—Determine the relevance of data to CI needs

—Eliminate false confirmations of data

—Provide feedback to other stages in the process

—Review and revise evaluation procedures in light of results, changes in operations, and feedback from other stages in the process

IV. Analyzing the Results

—Recognize patterns

—Seek out anomalies

—Identify and deal with disinformation

—Conduct supplemental collection efforts, if necessary

—Anticipate how a competitor thinks, based on what it has done

—Draw logical conclusions

—Provide feedback to other stages in the process

—Review and revise analysis techniques in light of results, changes in operations, and feedback from other stages in the process

V. Distributing the Results

—Format the results so that the information is readable, understandable, and useful to those to whom the information is to go

—Assure the security of the information

—Provide feedback to other stages in the process

—Review and revise distribution procedures in light of results, changes in operations, and feedback from other stages in the process

Appendix B
A CI Classification System

CI is like assembling a jigsaw puzzle in that you have individual pieces of data which can appear meaningless or insignificant, but, when assembled in the proper manner, they can produce a picture—valuable information. There are key differences between CI and jigsaw puzzles, among them that, when you deal with CI, you may have to remove some of the pieces and, with the pieces you keep, you should classify them as to their probable degrees of accuracy.

You may choose to develop your own system, or just to rely on hunches. But, as more data is collected and more people are involved in collecting it, you may find that you need some systematic way of marking individual bits of data to identify both its likely accuracy and the credibility of its source. One way is to use or adapt the following two character classification system.

Reliability of Source	Approximate Truthfulness of Past Reports
A. Completely Reliable	100%
B. Usually Reliable	80%
C. Fairly Reliable	60%
D. Not Usually Reliable	40%
E. Unreliable	20%
F. Reliability Cannot be Estimated	50%

Accuracy of Data	Probability of Truthfulness
1. Confirmed by Other Reliable Sources	100%
2. Probably Accurate	80%
3. Possibly Accurate	60%
4. Doubtful Accuracy	40%
5. Improbable	20%
6. Accuracy Cannot be Estimated	50%

DETERMINING RELIABILITY

To determine the reliability of a source of data, the original source of the data and the source from which you obtained it must both be considered. For example, current employees of a competitor may or may not be reliable sources of raw data depending on their attitudes toward their current employer as well as their perceptions of the use to which the information they are giving may eventually be put. Data from the suppliers of a competitor, even those with whom you also do business, may be influenced by conflicting factors, such as the desire to please, a reluctance to discuss other clients, or a lack of perception on the part of the individual providing the data.

The past performance, when available, of individual and institutional sources of data is generally the best basis on which to judge current reliability. A supplemental test of the reliability of the source is to consider whether, under the conditions facing the source, the source could have actually obtained the specific data within the source's limitations of time, access, and financing.

In applying the system outlined above, there are two guidelines which you may find useful:

1. If the source of the data is a friendly (that is one which is not presumed hostile to your interests, such as a competitor) and informed one, you can expect to assign an "A" rating when that source of data is known to have a long and extensive background with the type of data reported. The rating "B" would be assigned to a friendly, informed source which lacks the background experience, but is of known integrity. A rating of "F" is assigned when there is no adequate basis for estimating the reliability of the source. This might include, for example, information which has accidently come into your possession but which does not have a clear source, so you cannot evaluate the source at all.

2. If you get data from a unit or a contractor which is regularly collecting this type of data, whether it be a business information firm, such as Dun & Bradstreet, a market research team in your firm, or a competitive intelligence firm, rate this unit based on its current state of training and experience, in addition to rating the source which provided the data in the first instance. When the source of a piece of data and the collecting unit have different evaluations, only the lower rating of reliability should be given to the data.

In evaluating the accuracy of the data, consider the following guidelines:

—If it can be stated with certainty that reported data originated from a source other than that which already provided the data being confirmed, then the data should be classified as "confirmed by other sources," and rated "1."

—If, applying the same test, there is no reason to suspect that the confirming data comes from the same source as the data being confirmed, then you can consider it as "probably true," and give it a rating of "2."

—If your investigation discloses that the raw data, for which you have no confirming data yet available, is consistent with the behavior of the target as observed up to the present, the data received is "possibly true" and rated "3."

—You would classify as "doubtful," with a rating of "4," reported but unconfirmed data, the contents of which contradict estimated or known behavior of the target, as long as the data cannot be disproved by available data.

—Reported data, unconfirmed by other available data and contradicting experience, is classified as "improbable," and would be given a rating of "5." The same classification would be given to reported data which contradicts existing data already rated "1" or "2."

—If research on a subject reveals that there is no basis for allocating any of the ratings of "1" through "5," the reported data is then classified as "6," since its truth cannot be judged. The statement that a report cannot be judged as to its accuracy is preferred to an inaccurate use of one of the other ratings. However, you should always check to make sure whether you can apply the ratings "1" or "2." If either rating cannot be given, because of a lack of information on the target, the rating "6" should be given.

Remember that ratings of accuracy and reliability are independent of each other. For example, a highly reliable source may report data which, when compared with other data known to be true, appears to be improbable. Its evaluation would be "A-5." On the other hand, an evaluation of "E-1" could be given to data from a source of unknown reliability when, through confirmation from other, reliable sources, the data is determined to be of proven accuracy.

Appendix C
Competitor Analysis Outline

The following is a typical outline of the elements of an analysis of one or more competitors. It can also be applied to a defensive analysis of your own business in its competitive environment as described in Chapter 10.

Competitive Environment:

—Industry structure
—Number of competitors, product lines, and locations
—Market shares, sales, and profits
—Industry marketing, distribution, and pricing practices
—Expansion potentialities of competitors
—Important differences among competitors
—Barriers to entry and exit
—Potential entrants and future competitors
—Indirect competition

Products and Services Offered:

—Product lines and services currently offered

—History of key products and services

—Depth and breadth of products and services

—Analysis of new products and services offered, including market impact and impact on competition

—Level and consistency of quality control

—Experiences with recent new products or services

—Probable new products or services to be introduced/eliminated

Sales:

—Current and future applications of products and services

—Commercial, non-profit, and government sales

—Domestic versus foreign sales

—Geographic distribution of customers

—Key end-users and customers

—Channels of distribution and their strengths and weaknesses

—Seasonal and cyclical problems

—Probable future changes in marketing direction

—Historical data

Pricing Policies:

—Pricing strategy

—Who prices products and services and how

—Price levels and flexibility

—Credit, discounts, incentives, consignments, and other special pricing programs and policies

Sales Force and Customers:

—Type of sales force: in-house versus independent sales agents

—Organization of sales force: by product line, by geographic market, or by end-user

—Training, capability, and compensation of sales force
—Number of customers
—Distribution and concentration of accounts
—Analysis of largest or most important customers

Marketing:

—Market shares by product line, by geographic area, and by industry segment
—Marketing approaches and their current effectiveness: seminars, entertainment, trade shows
—Samples of advertising, literature, and other promotional materials
—Customer service policies and performance
—Probable future changes in marketing direction and timing
—Delivery and distribution
—History of questionable marketing practices

Personnel, Resources, and Facilities:

—Labor force: cost, availability, and quality
—Personnel turnover
—Facilities: locations, current performance, and potential
—Improvements or new facilities planned
—Raw materials: sources and availability
—Manufacturing and operating costs
—Joint ventures, minority interests, and other investments

Technology, Research, and Development:

—Current manufacturing methods and processes
—Types and levels of research and development, including current and projected expenditures
—Key patents and other proprietary technology
—Size and capabilities of research staff

—Dependence on current technology, and need for new technology

—Access to, use of, and dependence on outside technology

Financial and Legal Position:

—Financial reports

—Liabilities

—Short- and long-term borrowing capacities and ability to raise equity financing

—Sales margin, return on assets, and return on equity

—Profitability of key divisions, products, or services

—Projections of financial position over the next five years

—Identification of sources of financing, including duration and strength of the relationship

—Comparison of profitability, cash flow, and other key ratios with those of major competitors

—Type and status of major lawsuits and regulatory actions: probable impact on finances and reputation of company

Ownership, Control, and Management:

—Major shareholders

—Directors, their backgrounds, and other business relationships

—Corporate and management organization: formal and informal

—How decisions are made and who makes them

—Management style, abilities, weaknesses, and emphases

—New personnel and recent restructuring

—Depth, experience, and adaptability of management

—Capabilities and weaknesses in functional areas

—Corporate politics

Overall Business Strategies, Policies, Objectives, and Perception of Itself:

—Business philosophy and corporate strategy

—Targeted markets and market shares

—Targeted growth rates and financial objectives

—Policy towards joint activities

—Regulatory constraints

—Make/buy policies

—Technological trends and targets

—How strategy is made and then implemented and conflicting objectives balanced

—How the target company sees itself

Perception by Competitors and by Customers:

—Quality of product or service

—Pricing

—Marketing and service capabilities and reliability

—Management and organization

—Technological base and capabilities

Appendix D
Setting Up an Internal CI Unit

WHY HAVE AN INTERNAL CI UNIT?

During the past several years, there has been increasing interest among many corporations in creating separate internalized CI functions, following the reported examples of firms such as IBM, General Motors, Texas Instruments, and CitiCorp. The rationale is that the more formal the structure which is charged with producing CI, the better the resulting product will be. If approached properly, this can be true. Where such a unit has not been successful, there appear to be several reasons contributing to its failure.

One reason may be that the cost of creating such a new function involves set-up costs and operating costs much higher than those incurred operating under a more informal system, where information is obtained on an as-needed basis. In turn, this generally means management has failed to anticipate the full amount of such costs.

Also, creating such a new unit, specializing in CI, may result in organizational objections. For example, it may be perceived as a threat to existing units, such as marketing, planning, finance, and law. Also, creating such a formal CI unit sometimes can give rise to misconceptions by management, stockholders, and the public that the business uses "spies."

For such a unit to function properly on a company-wide basis, it must include within it individuals with direct experience in each area to be monitored, such as manufacturing, technology, finance, engineering, personnel, and marketing. Many companies have been reluctant to release skilled individuals from their positions to serve with a permanent CI unit.

MAJOR MANAGEMENT ISSUES

In establishing and managing an internal CI unit, there are a number of key issues which are unique to the creation and supervision of the internal CI function. We outline them below. Using this list requires that you make a decision on each point. There are no right or wrong decisions. However, you will probably only create management problems by the failure to make decisions.

—How visible should the CI function be, internally and externally? For example, should it be called a competitive intelligence unit, accurately reflecting its functions, or should it be given a more neutral, but less correct title, such as information support or corporate reference services?

—How should the work of the CI unit be allocated between inside personnel and outside sources? It is unlikely that an internal CI unit will be able to or that you will desire it to handle all of the corporation's CI needs. For example, using an outside source for CI may be appropriate only to handle peak work loads, or it may be considered as important in merger and acquisition transactions, when internal security of sensitive information may be an important consideration. The decision on when and what to contract out is more easily made at the beginning of the operations of such a unit, since any organization may see as a threat to its growth or even its existence efforts to contract out "its" work.

—How will the CI unit fit within existing corporate culture and pathways? For example, you will need to recruit persons with broad backgrounds in your corporation and in the industry to work with a CI unit. They are typically the very persons seen as candidates for rapid promotion and long-term development within the corporation in other areas. To attract them, you must avoid creating a dead-end position. That means that a promotion line from the CI unit must be established and a decision must be made as to where the unit is located and to whom it is administratively responsible. Typically departments such as marketing, business development, and strategic planning can all make a strong case for having the CI function report to them. The Chief Information Officer (CIO) may also be a logical candidate to supervise and direct a CI unit, given the CI unit's heavy reliance on information gathering and management, and its need to provide reliable support to a wide number of corporate functions, all of which may dovetail with the charter of a CIO.

—How do you plan to measure performance of this unit and of persons within the unit? If you expect the unit to be 100 percent accurate, you are actually asking for it to provide information and draw conclusions of such generality, breadth, and subject to such qualifications, as to be virtually useless. On the other hand, if you make clear that perfection cannot be expected from this unit, you may encourage it to take the small risks necessary to assure quality, useable output.

—How will this unit be supported financially? For example, should you back charge other functions for the work that this unit provides to them? Or will the unit receive its funds from the same sources that support planning, legal, and related functions?

OPERATIONAL ISSUES IN THE INTERNAL CI SYSTEM

At the same time that you resolve the major management issues noted above, you must also resolve a host of operational issues which are unique to the creation and operation of an internal CI system. Some of these arise out of the demands of the CI process indicated by the checklist above; others arise due to the need to have an internal CI unit function properly in support of and work closely with numerous other corporate units.

For the sake of brevity, what follows outlines the major operational issues of such a unit. This integrates the elements of the CI process, outlined in Appendix A, into the structural and management context.

I. Structure
    A. How visible should a CI unit be?
    B. How should work be allocated between an internal CI unit and outside contractors as well as between internal CI units and units such as market research?
    C. Is a staged development of an internal CI program appropriate?
    D. Make sure that management's expectations of the benefits of having an internal CI unit are reasonable.

II. CI Goals, Targets, and Priorities
    A. Decide who defines them and how
    B. Determine who needs what information and how frequently
        1. Separate those who need to know from those who just want to know.
        2. Will the information be by product, by competitor, by market, or by some combination?
    C. Limit the number of targets and establish priorities among them.

D. Establish if your needs are for qualitative information, quantitative information, or for both. For example, should the CI unit regularly produce estimates of what the company's competitors perceive the company is planning to do?

E. Decide how the goals, targets, and priorities are to be reviewed and modified.

F. Determine the form of the final CI product. Determine if there will be a need for regular updates of previous reports.

III. Collecting Raw Data

Potential sources for raw data include:

A. Internal—from those who receive CI information and from other internal sources.

B. Affiliates—such as agents or independent dealers.

C. External—electronic data bases and non-electronic sources. These can range from monitoring trade publications to conducting regular interviews with customers.

IV. Transforming Raw Data into Information

A. Where will the accuracy and reliability of raw data be evaluated—where it was first collected, at headquarters, or in both places?

B. Will the CI unit be able to call on other corporate functions for assistance in evaluation and analysis? On what basis?

C. Will you have to take measures to protect the source of some of the data? For example, if some customers have contributed to an analysis of a competitor, you may wish to refrain from identifying them by name in a report so that the observations they made do not come back to haunt them.

D. The analysis must evaluate both the usefulness and validity of the data as well as of the source of the data.

    E.   Determine if the data must be integrated with other data and/or with previous CI reports.

    F.   The final report should distinguish interpretations and extrapolations from CI information.

V.   Dissemination of CI

    A.   Decide who the consumers of CI will be, i.e., marketing, legal, planning, business development, personnel.

    B.   Establish procedures for the dissemination of CI. This information should be kept secure and in confidence.

CONCLUSION

Each business ultimately has to decide not whether it will develop CI for its own use but when and how it will proceed to acquire and use CI. An internal CI unit can be one option. Its creation and effective operation demands an understanding of CI as well as critical decisions on both management and operational issues before such a unit comes into existence.

Once management makes these critical decisions, an internal CI unit can function in effective support of many other critical corporate functions.

REFERENCES

Fuld, Leonard M., "Cultivating Home-Grown Spies," *Wall Street Journal*, March 17, 1986, p. 20.

Ghoshal, Sumantra and Seok Ki Kim, "Building Effective Systems for Competitive Advantage," *Sloan Management Review*, Fall 1986, pp. 49–58.

O'Riordan, P. Declan, "The Emerging Role of the Chief Information Officer," *Information Strategy: The Executive's Journal*, Vol. 2, No. 2, Winter 1986, pp. 8–11.

Risen, James, "GM 'spy center' dissects competition," *The Los Angeles Times* reprinted in *The Morning Call*, December 6, 1987, pp. D1, D3.

Vella, Carolyn M. and John J. McGonagle, Jr., "Spy vs Spy: Competitive Intelligence," *Information Strategy: The Executive's Journal*, Winter 1988, pp. 27–32.

Glossary

The terms below are defined in the context of competitive intelligence, on-line data base searching, and business planning.

Benchmarking: A process for comparing one company's operations against other firms both in and out of the market. Typically, the comparison is made with those firms believed to exhibit the most efficient operations.

BI: Business Intelligence.

Business Intelligence: The process of obtaining raw data on competitors for business decisionmaking. Not all data may be from public sources. This is one step in the CI process.

CI: Competitive Intelligence.

Competitive Intelligence: The use of public sources to obtain data which is then developed into information, generally on competitors and/or competition.

Competitive Scenario: An analysis of what one or more competitors can be expected to do in response to changes in market and other conditions affecting the activities of a particular company. The analysis is based on a profile of the competitor, including estimations of its intentions and capabilities, derived from a study of its past actions, and of the perceptions, style, and behavior of its current and future management. Each competitor's actions are measured against the same set of expected market conditions and changes.

Current Data: Data which deals with a relatively short period of time, centered on the present. Examples of this might be sales figures for the past three-month period for one competitor.

Data: Raw, unevaluated materials. They may be numeric or textual. Data is the ultimate source of information, but only after it has been processed and analyzed. See also Current Data, Historic Data, Macro-Level Data, and Micro-Level Data.

Data Base: Systematically organized data, stored in computer-readable form for ease in updating, searching, and retrieving.

Disinformation: Incomplete or inaccurate information designed to mislead others as to your intentions and abilities. This differs from fraud, which involves distributing erroneous or false information with an intent to mislead or to take advantage of someone relying on that information. The term disinformation has its origin with the Russian term 'dezinformatsia." When used in the arena of international politics, espionage, or intelligence, it means the deliberate production and dissemination of falsehoods, fabrications, and forgeries aimed at misleading an opponent or those supporting an opponent.

Espionage: Either the collection of information by illegal means or the illegal collection of information. If the information has been collected from a government, this is a serious crime, such as treason. If it is from a business, it may be a theft offense.

False Confirmation: When a second source of data appears to confirm the data from a particular source, but does not actually do so. Typically, this is due to the second source having received information from the first source, or both sources having received their data from one common source. They confirm each other not because both are correct, but because both have the same origin.

False Positive: When a test gives an erroneous positive result instead of the correct negative result. The result is an indication that the sought-for condition is present when it is not in fact present.

FOIA: Freedom Of Information Act

Freedom of Information Act: Federal legislation which requires that U.S. Government agencies provide information to the public on request. Some agencies make no charge for conducting searches under the FOIA. Others charge for the time involved and/or for the cost of duplicating files. Not all federal government records are subject to the FOIA. The most important exceptions include classified information, personnel files, and material which is confidential or proprietary in nature (if it was given to the government and marked as such).

Historic Data: Data which covers a long period of time. It is designed to show long-term trends, such as gross sales in an industry over a five-year period. This may include projections made covering a long period of years.

Information: The result of analyzing and evaluating raw data, reflecting both data and judgements. Information is an input to a finished CI evaluation.

Information Broker: A business involved in obtaining data on many subjects, including business subjects, from public sources. The sources relied on are exclusively or predominantly public on-line data bases. The data is obtained and provided without substantial screening or analysis. The term originated because such businesses were seen as "brokering" the raw data found in on-line data bases, by extracting it and reselling it to businesses and individuals not accessing such data bases themselves.

Intelligence: Knowledge achieved by a logical analysis and integration of available information data on competitors or the competitive environment which is either immediately used in or potentially significant to the planning process.

Intelligence Cycle: The process of collecting raw data, processing it into intelligence, and disseminating it to the end users. Each of these three phases may overlap with the other phases.

M & A: Mergers and acquisitions

Macro-Level Data: Data of a high level of aggregation, such as the size of a particular market, i.e., consumer electronics, or the overall rate of growth of the economy.

Micro-Level Data: Data of a low level of aggregation or even unaggregated data. This might be data, for example, on a particular competitor company's or division's profitability.

Mission Statement: A broad description of the business organization's purpose.

90-10 Rule: A business maxim which states that getting the last 10 percent of the data or information you are seeking may cost as much as or take as much time as did getting the first 90 percent.

On-Line Data Base: A computerized data base which can be accessed and on which searches can be conducted from another computer in communication with it. Typically this communication is over telephone lines.

On-Line Searching: Using a computer to locate specific information from an on-line data base while in communication with the data base. Such searching is usually done on a time-sharing basis.

Planning: A process by which the mission of a business organization is defined, its competitive strengths, including resources and liabilities, are evaluated, its goals are established, its alternative courses of action identified and selections made from among them, and the programs, projects, and tasks necessary to achieving those goals are determined.

Program: A broad course of action that contributes to achieving a specific goal. A program directs the development of necessary projects and tasks.

Project: A specific course of action consisting of one or more tasks undertaken to implement a plan.

PR: Abbreviation for public relations. In business, it generally refers to all information released to the public by the business through the news media or in speeches.

Reverse Engineering: The purchasing and dismantling of a product to identify how it was designed and constructed. This is done so that costs and quality can be estimated. In the case of non-patentable processes and devices, it can provide information on how to produce a competitive or substitute product.

SDI: Selective Dissemination of Information

Selective Dissemination of Information: The use of data bases to continually monitor identified topics by having preprogrammed search strategies executed on a regular basis. In some cases, the searches can be written and saved, with instructions to have them executed automatically by the data base supplier at fixed intervals, and the results mailed to the searcher. In other cases, it can refer to a researcher regularly executing the same search, over those materials most recently added to the data base.

Shadow Market Plan: An estimate of what a competitor is

planning in its marketing efforts and an estimate of its capabilities. This is based on CI developed about the competitor, including an estimate of its intentions. Those producing the Shadow Market Plan put themselves in the place of the competitor and attempt to duplicate what the competitor's market plan would be.

Shadow Market Planning: This is similar to preparing a shadow market plan, in that it involves an estimate of what a competitor is planning in its marketing efforts and an estimate of its capabilities. However, it is an ongoing process and also involves simulating what the competitor would do, given its capabilities, its personnel, its track record, and its perception of market conditions.

SIC Code: The Standard Industrial Classification (SIC) Code. This is a major statistical classification system used to promote the comparability of establishment data describing various facets of the U.S. economy.

Surveillance: A continuous and systematic watch over the actions of a competitor to provide timely information for tactical responses to the competitor's activities.

Target: A specified competitor, facility, activity, or market of intelligence interest.

Task: An identifiable action which contributes to the accomplishment of a project.

Annotated Bibliography

The following bibliography is intended to assist you in finding additional information about the subjects covered in this book. Please remember that there are also references at the end of each chapter, directing you to other more specific works. We have not duplicated citations found in Carolyn M. Vella and John J. McGonagle, Jr., *Competitive Intelligence in the Computer Age*, Westport, CT: Quorum Books, 1987.

The citation of any publication is not a recommendation or endorsement of any sort.

BOOKS AND BOOKLETS

"Business Planning," Small Business Consulting Practice Aid 6, New York: American Institute of Certified Public Accountants, 1986. A basic, hands-on guide to developing a business plan for a small business. It is focussed almost entirely on the business itself.

Carey, E. Raymond, "Marketing Strategy—An Overview," Harvard Business School Case 579-054, Cambridge: HBS Case Services, 1978. A sound, short overview of the issues involved in developing and implementing a marketing strategy, one of the most important of business plans.

Daniells, Lorna M., *Business Information Sources*, Berkeley: University of California Press, 1985 (revised edition). This is an annotated guide to selected business books and reference sources, prepared by a business school librarian. It can help develop leads for historical information.

Horowitz, Lois, *Knowing Where to Look*, Cincinnati, Ohio: Writers Digest Books, 1984. An excellent collection of tips on finding research sources.

Metlzer, Morton F., *Information: the Ultimate Management Resource*, New York: AMACOM, a division of American Management Associations, 1981. A thoughtful overview of the importance of information, including CI, in the modern corporation and the organizational and ethical issues surrounding the collection and use of information. While somewhat dated and out of print, it is worth locating and reading.

Radzik, Adam and Sharon Emek, "Techniques for Problem Solving," Washington, D.C.: U.S. Small Business Administration, Management Aids Number 3.010, 1985. A helpful outline of how to approach many sorts of business problems.

Sammon, William L., Mark A. Kurland, and Robert Spitalnic, *Business Competitor Intelligence*, New York: Ronald Press, 1984. A collection of essays drawing heavily on military intelligence analogies.

U.S. Small Business Administration, Management Aids:
"Business Plans for Retailers" (Number 2.020)

"Business Plan for Small Construction Firms" (Number 2.008)

"Business Plan for Small Manufacturers" (Number 2.007)

"Business Plan for Small Service Firms" (Number 2.022)

This is a set of brochures outlining practical tips and workspaces for developing business plans for specific types of businesses.

Vella, Carolyn M. and John J. McGonagle, Jr., *Competitive Intelligence in the Computer Age*, Westport, Connecticut: Greenwood Press, Inc., 1987. A primer on CI, stressing the importance of on-line data bases as a source of CI, but also introducing those not familiar with CI to a broad range of issues, including ethical and legal considerations.

ARTICLES

Ball, Richard, "Assessing Your Competitor's People and Organization," *Long Range Planning*, April 1987, pp. 32–41. An argument for the introduction of CI techniques into management practices in the United Kingdom.

Kreischer, John L., "How To Develop A Strategic Business Plan," *Business Digest of the Lehigh Valley*, October 1987, pp. 10, 12. A short article, featuring the author's list of "common mistakes in business planning." Number 9 is "misjudging the competition."

McGonagle, John J., Jr., "Getting Information Out Of The Federal Government," *Information Broker*, July/August 1987, pp. 1, 6–7. A how-to article describing how to call on the vast, but often hard-to-locate, resources of the U.S. Government.

Palesy, Steven R., "Implementing Strategic Planning Systems In Diversified Companies," Harvard Business School Note 9-580-049, Cambridge: HBS Case Services, 1979. A study of the shortcomings of "scientific strategic planning" in action.

Prescott, John E. and Daniel C. Smith, "A Project-Based Approach to Competitive Analysis," *Strategic Management Journal*, September/October 1987, pp. 411–424. A paper based on several case studies of the application of CI to operational problems. The framework may be applicable to some CI assignments at the strategic level, such as in corporate planning or new business development.

Prescott, John E. and Daniel C. Smith, "Demystifying Competitive Analysis," *Planning Review*, September/October 1987, pp. 8–13. An article debunking seven myths of CI, including that CI is costly and appropriate only for major decisions and that CI personnel are primarily information gatherers.

Index

About the Authors

CAROLYN M. VELLA is president and founder of the Helicon Group, Ltd., a think-tank style management consulting company which provides competitive intelligence services for corporations, government bodies, and private individuals. She is the co-author, with John McGonagle, Jr., of *Master Guide to Control of Corporations* and *Incorporating—A Guide for Small Business Owners*. She has published articles in a variety of management publications including *Bank Marketing Magazine*, and *Mergers & Acquisitions*, and has been interviewed by *Business Digest*.

JOHN J. MCGONAGLE, JR., is vice-president of the Helicon Group, Ltd., as well as being an attorney and an economist. He has also served with the President's Sector on Cost Control (the Grace Commission), 1982–1983. He is the author of *Business Agreements—A Complete Guide to Oral and Written Contracts* and *Managing the Consultant—A Corporate Guide*. He is the co-author, with Carolyn M. Vella, of *Master Guide to Control of Corporations* and *Incorporating—A Guide for Small Business Owners*, and has published numerous articles on business, competitive intelligence, law, and economics.